THE
FRICKEN MAP
IS
UPSIDE DOWN

Notes From a Spiritual Journey

CARRIE TRIFFET

ISBN-13: 978-0-9838421-7-0
(paperback)

ISBN-13: 978-0-9838421-8-7
(e-book)

Library of Congress Control Number:
2019915363

First published in the United States by

GJI

Gentle Joyous Industries
Beaver, Pennsylvania 15009

CONTENTS

ADDENDUM

THE EXERCISES

This is the disclaimer bit

Here is the spot where I declare right up front that I am not a psychology professional. Nor am I a medical professional. It's where I ask you to use your own sovereign wisdom to discern whether the following book is right for you at this time.

This is also where I ask you to be kind to yourself. To use common sense. You're the one who knows you best. The following book contains, among other things, meditation exercises to help you deep-dive into your own emotional, spiritual, and physical freedom. It offers an approach that is extremely gentle, yet undeniably badass. Is badass right for you at this time? Only you can say.

I do know this much: If you're currently on meds to suppress difficult thoughts, feelings or psychological conditions, this is not the path for you right now. This book champions an approach that is the opposite of suppression, and the journey it proposes would therefore not be ideal for you to embark upon at this time.

If you're physically ill, see the healing arts professional you normally would. Follow that practitioner's advice. And enjoy this book purely as a window on what can perhaps be. Use discernment in all cases, please.

Perhaps this book can act as a jumping off point to help you find great compassion and respect for the uniquely quirky, massively inconvenient *you* that you know yourself to be. Maybe the information contained in these pages will help you relax into the gift of wholeness. My intention is that this transmission (both energetic and written) will help spark within you a firsthand knowing of the divine self within.

Disclaimers aside, please enjoy this book. May the adventure of discovery be as wonderfully eye-opening and liberating for you as it has been for me.

Carrie Triffet
August 12, 2019

Between you and me

I would describe my spiritual evolution over the past three decades as an ever-expanding (and occasionally contracting) roller derby of living awareness: Messy. Circular. Highly entertaining, yet overall a bit brutal.

Maybe you can relate. Maybe now and then you, too, have found yourself sidelined on the bench, nursing an injury dished up with glee by one of your own inner self-saboteurs. And wondering why the evolutionary process seems so damn hard.

The short answer is, it doesn't have to be. The long answer is, it's taken me thirty-three years to find the short answer.

As the title and cover suggest, I speak throughout this book of a spiritual *journey*. As if we're actually going from one place to another, evolving from one state of consciousness to another over a span of time, in order to reach spiritual freedom. It isn't true. The truth of spiritual freedom is always right here-right now.

But realistically that's not how most of us experience it. For most of us, myself included, a certain amount of journeying from here to there seems essential, before we can know eternally timeless truth firsthand. For most of us there seems to be stuff in the way that blocks this 'right here-right now' knowing. And even though it's pretend stuff, it's still in the way.

So although a time-based journey doesn't actually lead to true spiritual freedom, I've personally found the trip necessary anyway. I wrote this book because my own recent explorations not only fast-tracked my spiritual journey—they profoundly cleared the way. As a result, that knowing of right here-right now truth has sprung to life, and is starting to flourish within me.

This book is, among other things, a real-time chronicle of my own rather astonishing journey of accelerated transformation and liberation. Like my other books, it also contains a number of related teachings interspersed throughout. Unlike any of my previous books, these teachings adhere to no established spiritual dogma or philosophy. I'm a free agent these days.

The transition away from established teachings wasn't an easy one. At the time, this process was slow, confusing and awkward. Some pieces of the established teachings remained radiantly relevant for me (and do to this day), but try as I might, I simply could not seem to arrange those individual puzzle pieces into a coherent picture; I couldn't seem to experience for myself the living truth these teachings spoke of. And yet I could be satisfied with nothing less.

The established teachings are brilliant, of course. And some people undoubtedly find spiritual freedom by following exactly where they lead. Ten years in, I had to admit I wasn't one of them.

Eventually I learned to keep only the puzzle pieces I found helpful and resonant, along the way picking up other, seemingly random pieces presented to me through divine inspiration. And thus gradually, piece by piece, I allowed the (magnificently non-random) jigsaw puzzle of my spiritual worldview—along with everything I thought I knew about my self—to be radically reconfigured by a divinely Loving hand.

And funnily enough, I now find myself gazing out upon the same magnificent vistas described so eloquently by those established teachings. It's only the route of travel I took that seems different.

The Fricken Map is Upside Down

Drop your maps and listen to your lostness like a sacred calling into presence. This place without a foothold is the province of grace.

~ *Toko-Pa Turner*

PRELUDE

MINING FOR GOLD

It's all fun and games until somebody loses an 'I'

With a toss of her head, the woman across from me flipped back the curtain of blond hair from her right eye. It was the sort of haircut designed for one-eyed living. The sort of haircut that would drive me mad if it were mine. She smiled warmly across the café table and regarded me with one-and-a-half eyes, her tresses falling right back into their preferred spot.

'Who is the 'me' that would be driven mad by this haircut?' She inquired patiently.

I sighed. It was my own damn fault. Steve and I had been wanting to broaden our circle of acquaintance. Genuinely fond as we were of the local villagers in our corner of the English countryside, we found ourselves forever feeling like exotic specimens, seemingly the only tree hugging, Source-loving, moonstruck metaphysical types in a ten mile radius. I guess we were craving the company of like-minded souls. People on a spiritual path.

Steve had recalled her name from the distant past, a woman who had once been active in the local non-dual Awareness community. With a little diligent research, I found her on

LinkedIn. As a job title, her profile had stated '*Living from pure Awareness*' or something like that. I had taken it to be an aspirational statement. As it turned out she really was living from pure non-dual Awareness, and had been for decades.

She was of that rare breed, one who suddenly becomes enlightened in the middle of doing algebra homework, or cleaning the litterbox, or whatever. One day she spontaneously woke up and all sense of a personal self crumbled away forever into the void. She still went through the motions of living a life, raising a family, holding a job. Yet no person was present for any of it. Nobody was thinking, yet thought was occurring. Nobody was making peanut butter sandwiches for a toddler, yet sandwiches were made. Life, in the shape of a soft-spoken woman with an asymmetrical haircut, was happening all by itself.

This complete loss of personal identification is seemingly the holy grail of the non-dual path, and for many years she had obligingly worked with eager seekers who hoped to experience for themselves that same stateless state. Even though, as she would tirelessly point out to them, there is nothing to experience. Experience is happening, but there is no experiencer.

Not unreasonably, she had assumed Steve and I had invited her out for coffee because we wanted some relentless non-dual pointing toward truth. In fact we invited her out for coffee because we like coffee. After a good hour and a half of no conversational statement left unchallenged—*Who is the 'I' that feels burned out? Burnout is simply happening*—we thanked her and made our exit.

That was a few years ago. A couple of years before that, I'd had a brief taste of the very truth she'd been pointing toward so patiently. Back in April of 2014, while wandering aimlessly through the walled city of Old Jerusalem, in the midst of overwhelming heat and hubbub, it happened. Without warning, the personal self, the personal Carrie, suddenly vanished.

I realized 'I' didn't exist. Had never existed. I was not the busy person immersed in highly important doings, that I had always assumed myself to be. I was, in fact, a figment of my own imagination. Surrounded by this noisy tourist throng, I knew myself only as an impartial and impersonal gap through which oceans of stunningly irrelevant Carrie-centric stuff had always poured forth.

My feelings, *my* worries, *my* passionate opinions about everything and nothing. *My* ideas about the spiritual path, and how it was supposed to unfold. None of it was real. None of it mattered. Only this majestic emptiness mattered. It stopped me in my tracks. I sobbed a little.

I'd been a seeker of enlightenment for a very long time. Some kind of dramatic shift in perception was exactly what I'd been aiming for, hoping for, all along. Not *this* kind of dramatic shift, mind you. This one sucked.

This one, adding to its other peculiarities, was only a partial shift of perception. One in which there was definitely still very much an experiencer. (Sorry, nice blond lady.) And the acute experience of sudden identity loss, coupled with the recognition that none of the things I cared about had any meaning at all—well, it was infinitely more disappointing than I'd bargained for.

The spiritual seeker part of me was thrilled to bits nevertheless, because on some level I recognized this impersonal spaciousness could lay the groundwork for the permanent inner peace I'd always sought. This part of me lobbied hard for making spacious emptiness our new home base. But the vast majority of me wanted absolutely nothing to do with it.

As with so many other things in life, when it comes to accepting an awakening opportunity, the majority rules. So the brief recognition of untethered grandeur faded as quickly as it came. In its aftermath my response was typical of the way I tended to view such awakening moments: I was bitterly annoyed with the part of the self that refused to get with the program. The foot-dragging part that always seemed bent on spoiling my heavenly fun.

For most of the previous decade, my focus had been on teachings of ultimate truth, beyond the limiting world of form. Pure, pristine divinity was all I was interested in. I had no curiosity at all about that mysterious 'silent majority,' no desire whatsoever to find out why this inner self might be choosing to lag behind. I had no patience, understanding or compassion

The Fricken Map is Upside Down

for life as viewed from its limited perspective. My spiritual roadmap simply didn't allow for that.

Years passed before I recognized the actual truth being pointed to so insistently, in that stifling hot Israeli marketplace. The non-dual awakened moment wasn't it. That moment of disidentification with the personal 'me' was only acting as the pointer.

The reluctant inner self it pointed *to*, I eventually realized, was the unlikely key to just about everything. In an altogether unexpected way, the inner foot-dragger turned out to be at the very heart and soul of permanent peace.

The evil genius

I didn't turn toward the inner foot-dragger comfortably or easily. Three decades of spiritual training had taught me to dismiss or overpower this reluctant subterranean self. The picture painted of this inner self by so many spiritual teachings was anything but flattering. Traditionally, most have considered this aspect of the self to be something of an evil genius, hell-bent on keeping us from knowing our own inherent divinity. All worldly suffering is blamed on it.

But here's the thing. For me personally, this kind of training didn't seem to fit my skill set. Try as I might, thirty-something years of hard effort brought little success in dominating or dismantling this stubborn portion of the self. Plenty of other nice things changed dramatically along the way, as a result of all the hard labor. But never that.

Yet that had long been my one great desire. To know my own inherent divinity. To radiate peace from within. But if these spiritual lineages were to be believed, I could never hope to know true peace as long as the evil inner genius was alive and functioning. *I should starve it,* they counseled. *I should kill it. Only then could I be happy.* Except in my case, the starvation diet simply didn't work. I was clearly outmatched.

Nothing I tried dislodged the evil genius from its core seat of power. Consequently, I couldn't seem to get anywhere near my desired destination of transcendent inner peace. In fact, every step I took in the direction of peace seemed to lead me father from it. Thirty-odd years into this journey, it finally occurred to me I was thoroughly lost—with no idea which direction might lead toward authentic peace.

For the first time ever, I stopped to take honest stock of my spiritual journey as a whole. If not toward inner peace (which at this point was clearly not happening), where was I hoping my path would take me? How, exactly, did my spiritual life, with its transcendent meditation practices and brilliant little awakenings, translate into my actual daily life—like, y'know, after the meditation was over?

As I launched into each day, was I feeling ever-greater inner fulfillment? Ever-increasing appreciation for life itself? Was I growing steadily more compassionate in my attitude toward humanity and its foibles? No? Okay, well was I at least becoming more gently accepting of my own imperfections? Was I increasingly happy just to be me? Uh. Not really. Not that either. *So then what,* I asked myself with a certain amount of exasperation, *was this all-consuming spiritual journey actually about?*

It was a pivotal question. In the unanswering silence that followed, I gave up trying to be my own navigator. I dropped my map and surrendered into the lostness that engulfed me. Like most forms of spiritual surrender, this one brought with it the immediate seeds of salvation, although I certainly didn't recognize that at the time. I didn't even think of it as surrender; I was merely admitting the totality of my failure, because it could no longer be denied.

I gave up control of the map—of all maps, now and forever. In my hands, I now realized, the fricken things were useless anyway. So I set aside all my training and everything I'd ever learned, along with all my preconceived judgments and ideas

The Fricken Map is Upside Down

about what my spiritual path was supposed to look like. And I let divinity reconstruct my navigation device on my behalf.

My attitude toward the ego self has transformed completely over the past two years. It has become abundantly clear to me it isn't evil in the least—even as I have also come to recognize just how correct all those established teachings really are, when they speak of its inherent God-blocking properties. The egoic perceptual lens *is* unquestionably the source of all suffering. Yet this aspect of the self can't help being what it is, and it believes its job is to keep us safe, no matter what. It does its best. For me, the appropriate response to its efforts is compassion for our shared plight.

This non-adversarial attitude has made it possible for me to work very powerfully with both the subterranean egoic self and the higher divine self. In this divinely led partnership, much has come to light. For one thing, I've been shown time and again that the unconscious mind is capable of far more responsiveness than is generally assumed.

Even if it is looping old patterns of pain over and over again, reliving its traumas in what seems a mindless or unconscious way, the simple introduction of *my* conscious awareness, *my* loving intention, was all it took to gently awaken this subterranean region to itself. You'll see some examples of what I mean, later on.

In exploring this part of the self, I've come to recognize there is great purpose, perhaps even great nobility in its function. The unconscious faithfully carries many heavy burdens on our behalf. Part of the spiritual maturation process, as I see it, is to learn how to help lighten that load.

I feel the whole idea of the ego could use a radical rethinking. I used to give lectures in which I sometimes worked with 'The Ego Puppet,' a googly-eyed sock puppet I wore on my arm. I used it to demonstrate (even back then) the ego is not a separate evil entity to be blamed for our ills, as it is so often portrayed in spiritual circles. I conversed with the puppet at length about its tireless efforts to do our own bidding. And finally I pointed out, to great guffaws from my audiences, that if you look carefully you will notice it's always been your own hand up the ego's ass.

My little standup comedy routine had its roots in truth, of course. The subterranean self is always trying, in its often head-scratchingly bass-ackward way, to do exactly what we're asking of it. To blame it for that is just shouting at the mirror. But I've come to realize I had my depiction all wrong. It is, in fact, the other way around. The subterranean self is not a puppet at the end of my arm. I am the puppet. And the subterranean self is the one who innocently pulls my strings.

Consider this. The personality self is often likened to an iceberg, right? The top ten percent is thought to be the conscious surface dweller, the one who answers when somebody calls your name. The so-called 'real you.' And the rest of the iceberg resides in the murky depths. All our wounds, unresolved issues and traumas reside there as burning hotspots. Most of the time we don't feel the burn directly; that's what the ice is for.

We only get a rush of heat when somebody or something pushes our buttons. Meaning, they've bumped into one or more of those painful unresolved hotspots. And when a hotspot gets activated, it flinches. It can't help itself.

This involuntary contraction automatically yanks on our strings, causing us, the surface-dwelling personality to jerk abruptly. Generally speaking it takes a fair amount of consciousness and plenty of practice, to be able to interrupt that knee-jerk reaction to an activated hotspot, because our strings are wired directly to it.

The more unresolved hotspots our submerged iceberg contains, the more reactive we are to inner and outer circumstances. Reactivity is pretty much the opposite end of the spectrum from true peace. When I finally realized true inner peace wasn't even slightly likely, it was because I saw this connection between subterranean hotspots and my own surface-dwelling experience of daily life. My iceberg contained deeply buried hotspots galore. I couldn't seem to get at them, but I sure as hell felt their effects every time they flinched.

The Fricken Map is Upside Down

Eventually I came to the conclusion that the submerged ninety percent is the one steering the ship—the one who is actually having a life experience that answers to the name on our birth certificate. The top ten percent is just the figurehead bolted to the front of the boat.

It was with this humbling recognition that I, the gaudily painted figurehead on the Good Ship Carrie, finally relinquished all delusional belief in my own independent power, authority and rightful role as captain. I saw, finally, it's never actually been me at the helm.

The half-acre I call home

What follows is a little more in-depth backstory explanation, leading up to that decision to turn away from everything I thought I knew. Because the decision itself was a pretty big deal. It felt radical. To abandon all spiritual teachings and concepts felt like I was trespassing upon a secret forbidden zone. The very idea of stepping beyond all known boundaries seemed like a violation of the rules, somehow. Somebody else might find such a thing exciting, but I'd never been the rule-breaking type; I did it only as a highly uncomfortable last resort.

Here then, is a brief rewind. A short history of my spiritual journey, and how it brought me to this choice point.

Thirty-something years ago I began my first spiritual practice as a way to fix my dysfunctional life and livelihood. I did it because I wanted to feel better. Career, relationships, finances, health, housing and just about everything else was in serious need of cleanup. If my life had been a parcel of land, you could have likened it back then to a stagnant, polluted swamp.

I worked hard in those first twenty years of diligent daily practice. As a result the muck and stink of the swampland slowly receded, leaving nutrient-rich soil in its place. Each time a newly fertile bit of soil revealed itself, I rushed in to plant beautiful flowers in tidy rows. Over the years my patch of land gradually transformed into a rather damn fine good-looking garden. The envy of many other would-be gardeners, in fact.

My dysfunctional relationships had become functional; serious illness had reversed itself completely; and I'd gradually gone from deep debt to savings in the bank. I had a good marriage to a good guy. A good career with good clients. A good house in a good town. Good friends. It was all very, very good, and I was deeply grateful for all that goodness. But. And.

I started to notice, no matter how carefully I weeded the unwanted debris and planted nicer things in its place, the ground underneath my little half-acre didn't feel good. Despite the lifelong desire for peace, inside I was anything but peaceful.

This had always been the case, of course. But so many more pressing things had been wrong with my life, the inner unease had barely registered. Now that the landscape was green and skies were patchy blue, I became unbearably aware of my uncomfortable inner condition.

Closer examination revealed my attractively landscaped garden was perched atop an abandoned mine, the tunnels dark and forbidding, the entrance long since caved in and sealed tight. It was then I realized I could pretty up the garden until the end of time, but my subterranean regions would remain largely untouched by that effort.

Naturally I assumed the tunnels and their unknown contents were the cause of my pain. If I could just get rid of them I'd be happy. Over the following decade, I tried to pry the tunnels open, flooding them with the healing Light of divinity until they cried 'Uncle.' Or sometimes I cajoled, offering sweet-talk and patient reasoning along with my heavenly searchlights.

The Fricken Map is Upside Down

Other times I lost patience, and went at the mine's entrance with a non-dual battering ram instead. Nothing worked.

Damn you, abandoned mine. Can't you see I want to fix you? Well, maybe not fix you. I want you gone, because you're blocking my access to enlightenment. Why won't you go away, so I can know inner peace?

No response. (Unless, of course, 'crickets' counts as a response.) For years, I nevertheless remained grimly determined to unleash the bulldozers, for an extreme makeover on my underground landscape. I vowed I would not stop until my garden smelled pretty inside and out.

Yet by and large, this collection of shadowy tunnels remained stubbornly unknowable and utterly immovable. The harder I tried to eliminate the entire subterranean mine—or better yet, bypass it with a jaunty wave, my heavenly jetpack propelling me up, up, up beyond the clouds—the more grimly it dug in. It wasn't interested in my little epiphanies and awakenings. It wasn't impressed with my spiritual illuminations in the least. Our rejection, it seemed, was mutual.

Enlightenment per se had never been my intended destination in those early landscaping days. A desire for awakened consciousness never even made it onto my radar screen, let alone my metaphysical bucket list, during the first twenty years of spiritual practice.

As far as I knew, a quest for enlightenment looked like that old cliché parodied in *New Yorker* cartoons. The cross-legged guru on a mountaintop, and the disheveled climber who arrives at long last to ask the guru his Big Burning Question: *What is the meaning of life?*

Um, right. I was no existential rock climber. Who cared what the meaning of life was? I just wanted to feel better. I had no concept of what we were supposed to be awakening from, or why enlightenment was even a thing. (Or a no-thing.) I just knew way down deep in my bones, somewhere, somehow it was possible to feel lasting peace. And that's what I was after.

It wasn't until my first brief ass-kick of a spiritual awakening in 2005 at the age of forty-seven, that I got an actual taste of that peace. It was transcendent. Big as the entire universe. My life restructured itself completely in its aftermath, this time with the map oriented firmly 'True North,' toward the direction I assumed enlightenment would be found.

Big changes had come in the powerful aftermath of that awakening. Over the next few years one good marriage ended, and another good marriage began. One good life in a beautiful Californian beach town was eventually traded for another good life in a beautiful English hamlet. It seemed, at first, like a huge evolutionary leap forward into divine trust. And in some ways it was. Yet deep beneath the surface, nothing changed. The abandoned mine and I remained at a stalemate.

It was clear this powerful subterranean intelligence wasn't going to budge if it didn't want to. Nor was it going to let me go anywhere without it. Inner peace simply wouldn't happen without its consent. *I* was the one, in the end, who cried 'Uncle.'

So I finally dropped all my 'spiritually correct' certainties. I dropped my arrogance. I dropped everything I thought I knew about maps, and tunnels and everything else. I let go of my withering judgment of this stubborn subterranean self, and took a closer look, this time with fresh eyes. Was it possible nothing about this old mine needed fixing? What if I was only seeing it incorrectly?

Setting aside all my ingrained assumptions, I began to comprehend at last the fundamental mistake I'd been making all along. This old abandoned mine was...*mine.* Maybe it was time to reclaim it. To treat it as something valuable, something dear to me. Maybe even offer it some long overdue respect.

For the first time I approached the tunnels and their mysteriously alive contents with complete humility. I stood at the mine's metaphorical entrance and quietly knocked. I asked to be allowed in, as a student who knew nothing.

I reached out to this much-maligned aspect of the self, even though I had long believed its sole desire was to deprive me of peace. I became genuinely curious to know more about it, to understand life from its subterranean point of view. With this change of attitude, I found my wish readily granted. Knocking on that symbolic door with full trust and an open heart, I asked for, and received, permission to come home.

Who knew such a simple shift would allow a breathtaking world of miracles to unfold? In equal partnership with all aspects of my self—from the very highest to the lowest—I soon discovered this reclaimed mine of mine offered an unlimited motherlode of inner exploration. And there was gold in there.

Earlier I was sure of so many things, now I am sure of nothing. But I feel that I have lost nothing by not knowing, because all my knowledge was false.
~ *Nisargadatta Maharaj*

ONE

My tiny guru

One day last summer, fresh out of the shower I sat down to meditate. I began by asking the question: *What it would take for me to Love humanity?* Not in the intellectual abstract, but, y'know, for real.

Because let's face it. We suck, right? We're a tough bunch to Love. And yet many times in meditation, I had experienced firsthand the God-self-ness of human beings, individually and collectively. I had felt our divine Light, our timeless innocence. *Where's the disconnect*, I wondered? *How do I experience this purity of self and other in my daily life?*

Just then an incredibly persistent housefly began buzzing and buzzing around me, landing periodically to tickle its way across my bare arms or zip back and forth around my wet hair. I smiled and acknowledged its God self, which of course meant nothing at all to the fly. He knew what he was. He was also thirsty and I was a bountiful fountain of recently show-ered moisture.

No amount of shooing had any effect at all. I tried slip-ping into conscious Awareness and meditating on the in-convenience of his behavior, seeing the behavior itself as God. Seeing my own mild annoyance as God. It's all true of course, but the buzz-tickle-stop, buzz-buzz-stop-tickle was

The Fricken Map is Upside Down

so random it would have taken a meditator far more masterful than I to manage it.

And yet I had long since realized everything arises as an opportunity to shepherd me along my path of awakening. So I checked in with my higher self: *Is there a lesson here? Does this fly have something to teach me?*

As if in answer, the fly turned and flew straight at the tip of my nose—*bop!*—with a force that startled both of us. *Okay, I'll take that as a yes. What am I missing? What's the lesson?* I paused to allow an answer to arise from the depths of divine inner wisdom.

I was invited to notice that greater vision, greater Light and greater Love are automatically limited by the habitual action of seeing through the lens of the personal self. I was viewing things from my own perspective. (Of course! Who wouldn't?) That perspective naturally included my own needs and wants: I wanted to meditate. Meditation was important to me. It's what I do, it's who I am.

Yet this fly, this outsider, was ruining my meditation because its own needs and wants were, of course, its primary concern. Were my needs and wants actually more important? Or were they just more important to *me*?

I wasn't really wondering whether flies should be accorded equal rights. I was asking this question to investigate my own egoic assumptions about life. I was beginning to notice my own agenda was not necessarily more important than anybody else's. It just felt more important because it was mine.

This was a question I'd pondered before, most recently while tending my garden. I was the one growing the veg at great effort and expense. What was the right attitude to take toward the beings who were busy decimating my lettuce crop? I couldn't bear the thought of waging war; that was the complete antithesis of where I wanted to be in my life. It was just too damn painful to cultivate enemies anymore.

I decided I valued inner peace more than I did my lettuce. I also valued peace more than I valued my ingrained assumption that my lettuce belongs to me. So I blessed these slimy little creatures, then plucked them off my leafy greens (ick) and repatriated them to the other end of the garden. They came back, and back, and back again of course, until no lettuce remained.

Bugs, birds, rodents, slugs. I was sort of willing to entertain the idea that I was not automatically entitled to harvest what I grew. And since all of Nature seemed to passionately and emphatically agree with that conclusion, I figured there must have been a lesson in there somewhere. But that was as far as I'd gotten on this particular question.

So this new bit of wisdom was highly pertinent to my daily life at this time. Although I had already been experimentally looking outside my me-centric ideas about life, it was still me doing the looking. The 'me' self was chewing over the idea of stepping outside the viewpoint of the 'me' self, in other words. I hadn't thought to examine the fact that the 'me' lens itself is the limiter of wisdom.

The higher self's implied suggestion was a delicate one: Why not play around with viewing the situation from beyond the limiting lens of the personal self? I realized this exploration would offer not only an answer to the housefly-meditation thing and even the garden pest conundrum, but an answer to the question I had posed at the start of the meditation. Where was the disconnect between the recognition of God in humanity I experienced during meditation, and the ability to apply that knowing to the actual human beings we are?

I immediately checked in with the personal 'me' self. Gone are the days when I would take a unilateral battering ram to its defenses in the name of spiritual progress. I was only too aware this suggestion of stepping outside the personal localized viewpoint, would strike at the very heart and purpose of the personal self. If I wasn't viewing the world through its subterranean lens, then what exactly was its job description?

What do you think, I asked. *Would you be willing to allow this exploration, to help me understand better?*

The fly's buzz-tickle-buzz-buzz antics had become too much at this point. I moved into the bedroom and closed the door. When I checked in again for the subterranean self's response, I realized I was feeling no inner resistance of any kind. It had quietly backed away, leaving me free to explore outside its usual boundaries. I was overcome with a wave of deep admiration and gratitude for the subterranean self's bravery and (ironically) its selflessness.

I'd been working patiently and steadfastly with the subterranean self for several months by this point. It had taken quite a while to build mutual trust and respect between us. Even though I had dropped all my jaundiced ideas about the intrinsically destructive motivations of the subterranean self before I approached it, I found myself unable at first to extend it my authentic trust, affection or respect. Even though I wanted to. Heartbreakingly, for its part, the subterranean self seemed far more eager to trust in me, far more willing to give me the benefit of the doubt than I could offer it in return. Progress, genuinely desired on both sides, was steady but painfully slow and awkward at first.

I'll include here a representative example of my early attempts to reach out humbly and sincerely to this aspect of the self, just to give you some idea of the collaboration's rocky beginnings. I was not in the general habit of writing letters to the subterranean self, but I found myself doing so as I sat down to pen this diary entry.

January 5, 2018
Oh, sweetheart. Can I call you that? I so want to be able to offer you my love. But when I try it feels fake, to you and me both. And I want to trust you deeply and completely, because I know you deserve it. But no matter how hard I try, something within us (within me) just won't go there.

It's tricky. On the one hand I know in my heart the teachings about you are correct. You do block out true peace. And that hurts. How can I trust deeply in anything that blocks out God? But I also know you're not to be blamed for that. I know you're not evil. I don't know how I know, but I do.

Maybe my feelings will change as I get to know you better. In the meantime, instead of love or trust, I'll offer you everything I can right now. My honesty. My loyalty. I'm here no matter what. I want to learn what you truly are. I don't know why you do the things you do, but I'm interested. Whatever you want to share with me, I'd be honored to learn. So let's start with that and see where it takes us. Okay?

On this sunny summer day six months later, as I found myself preparing to meditate from outside the personal viewpoint, my relationship with the subterranean self was already one of ever-deepening trust and mutual respect. By this time we were routinely working together with the divine Light of Awareness, and could clearly feel the rapidly growing inner illumination, clarity and wisdom that is a natural hallmark of such a divine partnership.

Having taken refuge from the persistent fly behind the closed door of the bedroom, I sat and prepared for meditation. Sinking deeply into present moment Awareness, I marveled at how remarkably easy it felt to step completely away from any sense of personal viewpoint. For the first time I could ever recall (other than during awakenings), the 'me' point of consciousness held no gravitational pull.

Since the 'me' perspective was temporarily deactivated, I took advantage of this gift by focusing on the truth of what is. *What does truth feel like?* I wondered. *How does it feel to see humanity as the Creator sees us?*

I tuned into the human collective. Without a personal point of view I found I was automatically free of my own assumptions, opinions, beliefs, judgments and even my innate preferences. None of that was relevant. None of it held any kind of energetic charge. I could sense my vision had become far less restricted than usual; I was seeing from a higher perspective.

As I brought the Light of Awareness inside the collective sea of humanity, I first felt it as a surging, clashing, chaotic sea of movement and change. Yet there was nothing alarming or negative about it. Resting here, I was startled to discover this turbulent sea was actually made of ecstatic joy. I was made of ecstatic joy.

I sank in deeper, beyond the surface level of constant movement, and settled at last into deep stillness. And in this hushed

The Fricken Map is Upside Down

and holy stillness, this sacred foundation of our shared humanity, I felt our true nature. It was made of ecstatic peace.

That was it. That's what I had been missing. God is the collective perfection of all-that-is, exactly as it is. It's the ecstasy of our human perfection, exactly as we are right now. I just wasn't on a high enough wavelength to experience it, until I stepped outside the localized viewpoint of the individual self. Until, you might say, my heartfelt desire to know God became (temporarily) stronger than the desire to see things my own way.

And yes. This new knowing of our collective perfection was still happening only in meditation, not in daily life. What can I tell you. Mine has been a gradual ascension; so gradual, my ears don't even pop.

A high-speed chase seen through backward binoculars

I was being taught to step away from my own personal view-point with good reason. For years I'd been exploring the theme of enemy consciousness (and how to live beyond it), because the flip side of that tug 'o war is true inner peace. I was learning that an enemy is only an enemy, because I have perceived it as such. But the human perceptual view-point is a freaky thing. It was slowly dawning on me that I probably shouldn't have been relying on it as an advisor in the first place.

A human being's perceptual lens can never be trusted as an accurate reflection of the way things really are. Your perception and mine are not clear, factual representations of what we see. They're made up of our own highly personal sets of prior associations.

Some of these associations are cultural or religious, others are supplied by the society we live in. Any of these may give the illusion of common ground with those who seem to share our general view. Education and family influences (or lack thereof) also play big roles in shaping perception. Our own personal prior historical experiences, paired with this mélange of tangled associations, inherited assumptions and unexamined group expectations forms the lens through which we interpret everything we see. It's all relative, and no interpretation is ever truly accurate.

To illustrate how it works, here's a small example of my own from many years back. I was driving through South Los Angeles one day with a school friend I hadn't seen in ages. We had just been to a trade show together, and were on our way to another appointment someplace deep in the garment district.

In that section of the city several freeways converge in a complex series of cloverleaf curves, the on and off ramps weaving under and over each other in every direction. It takes a fair amount of lane merging to get where you need to go. Jabbering excitedly with my friend about all the changes in our lives since we'd last seen each other, I barely noticed what I was doing.

The Fricken Map is Upside Down

Having made it safely onto our chosen freeway, a few minutes went by before my friend observed, 'Um, there's a guy who's been driving alongside us for a while now, and he keeps looking in the window at you.'

'Really?' I asked, my eyes on the unpredictable antics of drivers in front and behind me, 'What do you think he wants?'

'I dunno,' she said. 'But he looks pretty mad.'

I felt a cold stab of fear. Partly because my own prior associations had long ago led me to the conclusion that other peoples' anger was unsafe, and I should always tap dance my way to a state of mutually agreed upon harmony whenever possible. And partly because of another prior association: This was Los Angeles, famous around the world for the occasionally lethal effects of road rage. I prayed the guy wasn't carrying a baseball bat or a gun.

I stole a peek over at him. A very dark skinned man of powerful build glared back at me. *Oh man. Oh shit.* I had no idea why he was mad at me, but prior societal associations of mine made his anger a little bit extra-frightening.

I grew up in an economically depressed Rust Belt town in the 1970s, where racial tensions ran high. My junior high school years in particular saw semi-regular flashpoints of pent-up student frustration, the racial lines often clearly drawn. I never got beat up, back then or ever. But sparks and fists flew all around me with a certain amount of regularity.

Decades later, on this Los Angeles freeway, I couldn't help but filter an encounter with this angry stranger through that junior high school lens. It was automatic; it's how our minds process new information. I made that unconscious linkage instantly, and promptly broke out in a nervous sweat. For the next ten miles his car kept pace with mine while I steadfastly refused to look at him, fervently hoping he would get bored and go away. He didn't.

At last I reached my exit, dismayed to see he was taking it, too. He followed behind me for another ten minutes as I made my way to our destination. I pulled into the parking lot and he brought his car to a screeching halt next to mine. We got out of our cars and stood face to face, him shaking with rage, me with fear.

I braced myself. This was many years before I knew anything about empathic tendencies and what it means to feel other peoples' feelings; all I knew was, his anger tore into me like a hundred knives hurled straight into my body. But there was something else too, something besides outward-directed rage. And in a peculiar way it hurt even more.

'You cut me off,' he snarled. 'Like I wasn't even there.'

Like I wasn't even there. That was it. A focused pinpoint of white-hot searing torment, aimed with surgical precision not at me, but at himself. Although I had no words to describe the phenomenon back then, I felt his inner pain and frustration for one blinding instant as if they were mine.

His momentary jolt of fear as I'd cut him off on the freeway (a normal reaction to being put in danger), had quickly turned to boiling fury at my apparent cavalier disregard for his inherent right to exist. (Instant linkage.) How dare I think his life was worthless?

I listened quietly, looking into his eyes as he spoke. When it was my turn to talk, I apologized humbly for my error, explaining truthfully I never even saw his car. It must've been in my blind spot, and I wasn't paying nearly enough attention to what I was doing, I admitted. I was genuinely sorry for taking him so many miles out of his way just to speak with me, and I said so.

He nodded, processing this new information. As I watched his face, I could see it was almost as if his inner GPS unit had originally taken him down a well-worn route marked 'Favorites.' But now it was recalculating an entirely different pre-programmed route. A route called 'Lady Drivers.' This road held no rage, just an exasperated handful of patronizing gender assumptions. He sighed heavily and turned away.

'See that you don't do it again,' he instructed almost offhandedly over his shoulder, shaking his head with a sour grimace as he pointed his car back in the direction he had come.

My point here is not to suggest his prior experiences of life weren't real. Or that his conclusions about his experiences weren't accurate. Of course they were. They were valid and

The Fricken Map is Upside Down

real to him, as my prior experiences were valid and real to me. It's the way we each pasted those historical assumptions onto our present circumstance that highlights just how unreliable and arbitrary the personal perceptual lens really is. By seeing through the lenses of our separate histories, we each brought wildly divergent and completely irrelevant ideas to the interaction. And because we believed what our separate lenses showed us, we each perceived ourselves as the potential victim of the other one's intentions.

It's the inner satellite navigation system itself that can't be trusted. It can never be relied upon to give an accurate reading. By analyzing its millions of data points to formulate its conclusions, that very process guarantees every road it takes us down will be faulty. Our inner GPS unit does its very best to help us navigate our world, bless it. But in truth, all of its data points are meaningless. And the destinations even more so.

Learning to take the personal point of view with a large grain of salt is fundamental to spiritual and emotional freedom. Strangely enough, I didn't fully recognize the deeply flawed nature of my own (or anyone else's) personal point of view, until my softened stance toward the ego self helped me notice firsthand the fallibility of its perceptual lens. The egoic lens just isn't built for accuracy.

I realized then that I am endowed with a personal viewpoint, simply because that's what allows me a sense of being a separate personal self. Not because there's anything inherently true or right in my way of seeing anything. So my egoic lens isn't worth a lot. And honestly, that personal self business? It ain't what it's cracked up to be.

God and creation

My new, insider relationship with the subterranean self was the first and most obvious change to my spiritual worldview. Yet it wasn't only this softened attitude toward the egoic self that characterized my gentler, post-map landscape. I also found myself embracing a different sense of God, and the nature of creation. A different sense of why we're here.

I didn't actively go looking for a replacement definition of God, or a different creation story. This wasn't an intellectual decision; it was done on my behalf, through divine grace. It forms part of the new navigation system, which arose from the spacious ground of not-knowing.

The ground of not-knowing, allows room for a perfectly customized, divinely-inspired journey to unfold—one that's exactly right for each individual journeyer. It's what happens when you clear the slate of what you think you know, and instead let your higher self reconfigure your spiritual navigation system. The puzzle pieces that make up your perfect spiritual worldview may or may not be the same ones as mine. They will be the ones that lead swiftly and gently to your own liberation.

The customized spiritual navigation system I describe throughout this book has been perfect for my own evolution. It has lifted me beyond my stuck places with ease and grace. That doesn't mean my spiritual worldview is universally better. It's just what's been perfect for me.

My revised sense about God and creation arrived without fanfare; these particular puzzle pieces quietly inserted themselves into my worldview over the last couple of years, and for me they're a good fit. They form the living foundation for much of what has occurred since.

I'll explain the update with a brief review:

When non-dual teachings speak about God, the infinite mystery of pure void is what they're referring to. Pure void is sometimes described as infinite, eternal emptiness. Which, paradoxically, brims with the latent potential for all-that-is. 'The Absolute' is another, possibly less confusing label for it.

This great emptiness-in-fullness can't experience itself. It cannot stand apart from itself, to perceive or experience anything.

But not everybody agrees on this 'prior to all that is-ness' as the definition of the word 'God.' Not everybody traces God that far back. And this is where creation comes into play.

Here is the creation story I find resonant at this time: The Absolute chooses to experience its own great infinity. To facilitate this, a 'deputy' of sorts arises out of the emptiness-fullness, and is tasked with carrying out this choice. The deputy is itself made out of three intertwined raw materials of divinity. These are Love, Light and conscious Awareness.

Employing these same three raw materials as fundamental building blocks of creation (because no other raw materials exist), this deputy creates all-that-is. All that can ever be. Creation is the deputy's principal function, therefore the deputy can accurately be called the Creator. And the Creator is what many people, not surprisingly, think of as God. It's what I think of as God.

The word 'Source' can also apply here. The deputy is the Source of all that exists. Or you could just refer to the deputy by its component parts: Love-Light-Awareness. A lumpier title, but technically accurate. Although I suppose it's a little like saying, 'Please pass the bottle of tomato-vinegar-spices,' when you really mean ketchup.

I'll be using the word 'God' interchangeably with 'Creator' or 'Source,' to mean the aforementioned deputy facilitator of the Absolute. And as you'll see throughout this book, the creation story described above (we are created so the Absolute can experience itself) is woven deeply throughout my own journey of the past couple of years.

TWO

Seeing clearly

One night a number of years ago, I was sincerely asking to see how God sees. I truly wanted to be able to look upon the world I live in, and find it innocent and holy. But it wasn't happening. Not even a little bit. So I was praying, asking for some kind of pointer that would help me make this shift of perception.

You know everything about me, God. My thoughts, my beliefs. You're there when I fart. You've seen me have sex. But I know nothing about you. Give me a hint. Show me how you see things. Help me know you better so I can see the world as you do.

Cute, right? Like I said, it was a long time ago. Anyway, I went to bed after that and slept as I normally would, dreaming about nothing in particular. But I woke in the early morning with a strong sense I was in the presence of a huge intelligence of some kind.

It was vast, deep and immeasurably powerful. I wasn't alarmed by its size or power, because it felt thoroughly benign. More than just benign—it was wholly suffused with the innocent sweetness and radiantly gentle spotlessness of God. This being, I realized, was Love and Light incarnate. And because it was all of these magnificent things, I could feel within my own mind-body-energy field that I was all of these things, too.

Yet I was puzzled. I felt I really ought to recognize this massive entity. It seemed so famous, so well known. I couldn't quite place it. Slowly the realization dawned: *Oh. My. God. This is the devil.* I was witnessing Satan—as viewed through a completely pristine mind. Satan, seen from God's perspective.

I'd been asking to see how God sees. This is how God sees. This is what unconditional Love-Light is. Everything is made of God, which means everything is witnessed and experienced by God *as* God. Everything is recognized as the pristine perfection it really is in truth, no matter what sort of havoc that perfection may be busy inflicting upon the world. Small wonder I was having such a hard time, trying to embrace this whole Love-Light-Awareness thing, eh?

The lesson provides a useful illustration of our shared human dilemma. If we want to know Light and Love as our own true identity, we can't be dabbling in exclusionary thinking. It's all or nothing; everybody or nobody. If we deny the divinity in anyone or anything (no matter how badly they may behave), we deny it in everyone and everything.

As if that prerequisite is not challenging enough, we have yet another hurdle to consider. To experience Love and Light as who we really are, we have to be on a similar wavelength to it. We can't be invested in fearful anxieties about the future, or caught up in believing stories about our own unworthiness, because those ideas all reside on a different, more knuckle-dragging frequency level.

Only in the past few years have I come to appreciate the role of energetic frequency and vibration, as it relates to spiritual evolution. Unconditional Love and Light are extraordinarily high frequencies, and if our mental-emotional activity is not a reasonably good match to these frequencies, we haven't a prayer of knowing those transcendent states firsthand.

And yet life on this planet inspires pretty much every one of us to work overtime, creating fearful defenses and limiting stories about ourselves and each other. We worry and fret, we judge and condemn. We fill our wounded hearts with fire and ice, or other numbing agents. The inevitable result, is that our personal wavelength rarely comes within spitting distance of the extremely high-frequencies where divine Love and Light reside.

*   *   *   *

If you are spiritually gifted or exceptionally lucky, your angelic guides might now and then offer you peekaboo glimpses of the mind-blowing beauty of your own true identity. For years I fell into the category of the very lucky, an enthralled tourist snapping pictures of my own magnificence from the safety of the tour bus. Yet I could never seem to own what was being shown to me. It was far too bright.

A visit to a heavenly tourist attraction is a wondrous gift for anyone to experience. It's not even slightly mandatory, however, along the spiritual journey. I have also come to realize it's not remotely the same thing as experiencing our own true Love-Light identity for real. I brought back only postcards and souvenirs, when I visited via tour bus. But I come back forever transformed by Love-Light itself, each time I'm able to own it directly—even just a little bit—as my true identity.

I bring this up only to point out how peekaboo glimpses differ from authentic embodiment of Love-Light, because I myself didn't understand the difference for many years. I could never figure out why my cherished collection of Polaroid Love-Light snapshots refused to develop into fully embodied knowings of divine truth.

Now I realize, in order to give us these careful tastes of our own divinity, our guides put up helpful screens and veils so we, the lumpy, carbon-based physical entities we are, don't burn to a crisp in the presence of our own glory. It's a kindness, in other words. And (despite the impatience of eager tourists like me) it's very necessary, until it isn't.

If Love and Light were forced upon any aspect of the self that actively doesn't want them, or isn't ready for them, an epic clash of wavelengths would ensue. Love and Light would then be experienced as a brutal spotlight interrogation at best, and incineration at worst.

The Fricken Map is Upside Down

And this is why Love-Light-Awareness waits so patiently to be authentically invited in. Not just by the conscious top ten percent of your ego iceberg, but by the other ninety as well. The cellular you, the physical you, is the determined secret keeper on your behalf. It would shriek with pain and terror if confronted prematurely with the unlimited, unflinching Light of divine truth. And Love-Light-Awareness wishes always and only to be kind.

Love and Light can only be fully embodied by an awakened, undefended heart, powered by the high-wattage energy field that is part and parcel of this divine state of being. Yet life on Earth does not exactly seem to lend itself to this kind of extreme attainment. So is the Love-Light divinity deck purposely stacked against us? I don't know. Maybe.

These days, I prefer to regard life on Earth as an epic virtual reality game. Each time we start from zero, with no memory of earlier wins or losses. The point of the game seems to be to load ourselves up with as many obstacles as possible, and then see how long it takes to remember ourselves as God.

From the standpoint of a divine being (which you are), there would be no advantage in remembering yourself too easily. Where's the fun in a game in which every roll of the dice predictably brings you closer to your guaranteed win?

More to the point, if our reason for being is to experience as much as we can on behalf of the Absolute, we will set up the game to be as nail-bitingly interesting as possible. Will she release her crippling fear of intimacy? Will he find peace within the morass of alcohol addiction? Success is never certain, from our limited perspective anyway. And that's what makes it such a kickass game.

No virgins were harmed in the making of this miracle

Along with the revised sense of God and creation, came a new appreciation of the energetic universe itself. As with God and creation, I didn't go looking for new ways of understanding the cosmos. These puzzle pieces were quietly dropped into my spiritual worldview on my behalf.

Even though it now embraces physics (meta, quantum and astro) to some degree, my spiritual worldview is also one of awe and wonder. I seem to have a newfound appreciation for the miraculous nature of existence itself. My core definition of 'what is a miracle?' has changed, and the quasi-scientific framework, for me, only adds to its profound beauty and mystery. So let's talk about miracles. What they are, what they're not, and perhaps have never been.

Modern culture tends to look back on ancient civilizations with a sort of bemusement at what we consider their child-like naiveté, or superstitious approach toward spirituality. We shake our heads at their efforts to appease the Gods Out There, in order to insure a good harvest, or make a plague go away. *Silly ancients*, we tell ourselves. *Good thing we're so much more sophisticated now.*

But it strikes me that our modern approach is really not so different, minus the odd blood sacrifice here or there. Occurrences we interpret as evidence of the spiritual realm in action (i.e. miracles), are really more like impartial displays of the structural laws of the universe.

Various branches of science speak of the existence of multiple dimensions, the first four of which together describe the recognizable laws of space-time as we experience them here on Earth. Some scientists cite evidence for six or seven more dimensions beyond those, or however many more they can measure with instruments, or postulate as suggested by mathematical probabilities. Metaphysical teachings, however, allow for a virtually infinite number of dimensions, each one related to an equal number of possible timelines.

The Fricken Map is Upside Down

You know the virtual reality games we've been talking about? This infinity of dimensional timelines explains the mechanism through which these richly complex illusions of life can exist. The direction of any given game can never be definitively known in advance, because endless moment-by-moment possibilities exist for any outcome. A grand game indeed, and one befitting the divine beings we are.

I've heard the mechanism described the following way. For what it's worth, this simplified analogy feels accurate to me in its basic explanation of how multi-dimensionality works, in relation to the life experience of any given gamer:

Your individual game of life is like an old-fashioned slide carousel (ask your parents), which is, in turn, hooked up to a slide projector. Although there are indeed infinite slides to choose from, some events (slides) are pre-programmed into your individual carousel before you start the game. Yet how you respond to each slide as you see it projected onto your screen, is entirely up to you. Your choice of responses, essentially, is the game.

That's because your response to the projected image is what determines which new slide will tumble in next from the vast universe of possible slides, to take the next slot in your carousel. How divinely aligned (or misaligned) was your reaction to the last slide you saw projected onto your screen? How high or low frequency was the nature of your response? Whatever it was, you will magnetically attract a slide that is its vibrational match. And your game will move seamlessly into that new direction.

So a miraculous healing (to swing back around to the topic of miracles—we do get there eventually), does not occur because you had an illness, then you prayed, and the next minute that illness was miraculously healed. Technically speaking, there's no such thing as a healing, miraculous or otherwise. It's just that your beautiful heartfelt prayer lifted you into a higher-vibration alternate timeline. One in which that particular illness doesn't exist in your body. In some other timeline, the illness continues unabated.

We're sliding between timelines all the time, but it's usually quite seamless, with only minor changes. Our bodies tend to age imperceptibly from one day to the next, for example. Each of the body's minor physical changes inhabits its own timeline. We don't pay much attention to the subtle, seemingly linear progression from one of these timelines to the next, because the small changes are considered normal and expected.

Bigger shifts, like the sudden disappearance of an illness, are noticed and labeled miracles. Out of the ordinary shifts like these clearly demonstrate in fact, timelines are under no obligation to behave incrementally or linearly. Dimensional timelines act like a bunch of random slides, and any one of them can fall into your carousel at any given moment.

They only seem to create small linear changes most of the time because that's what we expect. Large anomalies are called miracles because they defy our expectations of what is possible. We therefore tend to attribute them to the intervention of external deities.

But they are the result of connecting with your own inner deity—the one who has always known its own true divine identity, and knows perfectly well how multi-dimensionality works, even if you don't. The shift to another timeline is not the miracle. You, gloriously multi-dimensional you, are the miracle.

I'll give you a couple of my own relatively trivial examples of timeline shifting, based on high-vibrational responses to external stimuli. I have hundreds of similar examples to draw from. Suffice it to say I wholeheartedly embraced the above explanation of malleable timelines and dimensional possibilities when I encountered it, because it so closely matches and explains phenomena I've been experiencing for many years in my own life.

Here's the first example. Back in 2005, a few weeks after that first powerful awakening episode, I was invited to attend a client's annual general meeting and give a presentation to board members. This annual gathering was a three-day event held at an all-inclusive luxury resort in Cabo San Lucas. The resort boasted half a dozen immaculate blue swimming pools, including the de rigueur swim-up bar. Because God forbid you'd have to towel off before refilling your drink order.

I was still kind of buzzing with *I-am-the-universe-itself* Awareness after that initial awakening. So after a day or two of drifting around the various pools inside the resort complex, I decided it might be nice to wander down to the beach and have a solo experience of actual Nature.

One could see the beach from the resort but nobody seemed to go there. It felt oddly forbidden, almost, to leave the perimeter walls of the compound. As I stepped beyond the outer boundary I discovered there was actually good reason for that. They must've been using some kind of invisible electronic fencing to keep the bugs out.

The moment I stepped past the walls, time seemed to slow and I sensed the attention of thousands of bugs all turning to zero in on me. Uh-oh. Half a second later the cumulative buzzing filled my senses as I felt myself surrounded by ravenous airborne creatures, the first few giant welts already starting to form on my arms and legs.

But then all by itself, a knowing arose from someplace within me. With complete authority I silently said to the insect hordes, *I am sacred. I am not an appropriate food source for you.*

Everything immediately stopped in mid-buzz, and all bugs disappeared, along with the welts already existing on my body. At the time I didn't know whether to be more startled by the self who rose up out of nowhere to make that proclamation, or by the bug-free miracle it seemingly caused.

I had no explanation for the miracle at the time. Nowadays, I would say the divinity-assisted proclamation of my own inherent worthiness brought me into closer vibrational alignment with divine truth. I was seeing a bit more like the Creator sees. And this high-vibrational state shifted me into a timeline where that particular beach held no flying bugs.

Funnily enough my next example is also about bugs. I'm new to organic gardening, and I wanted to try growing cauliflowers. I knew it wouldn't be easy because so many different kinds of critters are incredibly fond of them. To make it even more interesting I wasn't content with just going organic; I wanted to try growing them in accordance with our no-kill/no enemies policy. So there would be no bug murder going on here.

It soon became obvious it would be a small miracle in its own right if these plants survived long enough to actually produce a head of cauliflower, because the beautiful blue-green leaves themselves were so desired by so many. Every day I would pick off, or spray water off, at least six different kinds of invasive insect. I didn't want to hurt them, just remove them from the plant. I kept infestation at bay, and as long as there were only a few of each type of bug I found it easy to remain loving while I did it.

About seven weeks into the process we took one evening off to go to a music festival, so the cauliflower plants went forty-eight hours instead of twenty-four without my usual attentions. I came back the following day to serious infestation—and every gardener knows how hard it is to reverse an infestation after it's already established, no matter what methods you use.

Some creatures eat a multitude of pinprick holes. Others, given the chance, want to eat the whole plant down to the stalks. And then there are the ones who simply prefer to suck the life out of the veins and stems. Still others like to lay their eggs on the leaf's underside, to give the caterpillar hatchlings a delicious buffet lunch before turning into winged things themselves and repeating the cycle. Most of the more mature leaves were hearty and strong enough to withstand the multi-pronged attacks, but I was dismayed to find many of the younger, smaller leaves had been decimated.

A number of these vulnerable baby leaves now held eggs, three or four types of bugs and tiny newborn caterpillars in addition to having already been eaten down to lacy stalks. I was surprised to notice myself becoming a little bit angry and indignant on behalf of these defenseless baby leaves. *It wasn't fair*, I thought, *that the innocent babies were getting attacked from so many quarters, when they were obviously too young and tender to defend themselves.* And I noticed I got a little bit ruthless in my bug and egg removal. They had, in some small way, become my enemies.

Many weeks earlier I had relinquished my expectation, or right, to an actual cauliflower harvest. I had been asking very pointedly for some time, to be shown not only how to correctly witness 'enemies out there,' but also to know how to properly behave in response to their transgressive actions. Not just in my garden, but also in the world I perceived outside me. I had watched the cauliflower leaves attracting transgressors and (much the same as while losing my lettuce) I realized right away if forced to choose, I'd far rather learn this lesson about enemies, than harvest cauliflowers. Even though we really like cauliflowers.

I was already pretty good at knowing there's no such thing as an enemy in truth. But what about taking action at times it's clearly needed, whether here in the garden or in more extreme cases out in the world at large? Was I just supposed to think spiritual thoughts and look the other way? That answer didn't seem quite right, in the chaotically transgressive age we live in. *Was it ever appropriate to take a stand against transgressors*, I wondered? *Sometimes action is surely required. Isn't it?*

I knew my cauliflowers and their many devoted admirers were here, in part, to teach me about this larger issue, surely one of the most urgent lessons of our time. So my antennae went up immediately when I noticed I was becoming angry at the unfairness of the relentless attacks upon innocent babies. I correctly identified this interpretation as my own subterranean 'enemy generator' at work. I didn't buy the propaganda.

On the other hand I didn't embrace the lesson right away, either. I didn't fully dive into the opportunity clearly being offered, even though I'd been asking for this all along. After all, action was required first, right? The little buggers were everywhere. So I acted.

For two days I used three times as much water as before, grimly blowing the insects off the leaves over and over. They hopped right back on, of course. But I made sure I disrupted their nest building efforts, and slowed down the creation of colonies. If one or two of them drowned in the process, I wasn't all that sorry.

On the third day I sprayed the insect hordes off the first couple of plants, as I had been doing for the past two days, acutely aware of the futility of the exercise. It was only then I admitted to myself, I hadn't bothered to give full consideration to the lesson at hand. I hadn't yet taken it seriously enough to base my actions upon it. Recognizing I had little to lose at this point, I paused as I approached the next group of cauliflower beds, sprayer in hand, and chose to view all the living beings in those beds as being equally of God. I persistently basked in their Love-Light divinity, keeping at it until I could clearly feel my own.

I felt the telltale softness, as everything in my world now became imbued with the gentle glow of divinely illumined Awareness. And then I lifted the first leaf of the next cauliflower plant in line to be sprayed. It held eighty percent fewer bugs than the plants I'd sprayed a minute ago. The rest of the plants showed roughly the same degree of reduced infestation. Somehow I wasn't surprised.

I suppose it qualifies as a small miracle. Yet I prefer the metaphysical explanation, which seems to fit better: I brought the electromagnetic patterns of my thought-forms into more coherent alignment with the much higher-frequency patterns of divine truth. I thought a bit more like the Creator thinks, if you prefer that wording.

As a result, my own overall frequency lifted higher, which popped me, quite seamlessly, into a dimensional timeline that was a vibratory match for my own more divinely aligned frequency. A timeline in which the more devastating degree of infestation hadn't ever occurred. Or maybe it was a timeline in which other predatory bugs had already found the leaf-eating critters, and had obligingly hoovered up eighty percent of them.

That might be the more logical timeline explanation, because the plants' leaves were still every bit as damaged as they'd been before the timeline shift. If the infestations had never occurred, it would stand to reason the leaves would also reflect far less damage. That would've been awesome, to witness a garden full of cauliflower plants suddenly restored to their formerly pristine blue-green beauty and vitality. It would've been a sparklier miracle for sure, than the somewhat more prosaic marvel I experienced.

It would have more closely resembled the first example I gave you, of the already existing mosquito bites on my arms and legs that disappeared along with the mosquitoes, on that Mexican beach. In that earlier instance, I received a little turbo-charged boost of divine knowing. Undoubtedly that's what helped shift me into a super high-vibrational version of that beach moment.

Back to the cauliflower leaves, had I been utterly convinced of the Godliness of all plants, all leaf-eating bugs and myself alike, my own frequency might have risen to such an extent I would perhaps have attracted a substantially higher-frequency slide, or timeline, into my carousel—one in which no harm had ever been done. As it was, my sincere witness of joint Godliness fell within the realm of an enthusiastic exercise. Hey, I'm not complaining about the timeline result I got, by any means. I'm just saying, there's always room for improvement.

The next evening I paused before spraying, as I had done the day before, and felt more deeply into the holiness of all the bugs and cauliflower plants alike. This time I found the incidence of bugs was nearly nonexistent, lower than it had been before the infestations ever began.

This example of the cauliflowers may seem trivial (and I suppose it is), but it does point toward a couple of very powerful clues about the correct response to transgressive actions taken by 'enemies out there.'

One: Correctly aligned thought patterns that contain no trace of enemy consciousness, *even while in the midst of taking physical action to stop aggressors*, bring infinitely more powerful results than taking those same actions while perceiving the other as an enemy.

Herein lies the mystery, or the magic, or the miracle, or whatever you want to call it, of taking appropriate action while refusing to perceive enemies. Our own higher frequency, stemming from our more closely aligned action, inevitably must result in higher frequency outcomes than we could have ever imagined.

Like this one, for instance: As I was finishing with my cauliflower chores on that first day of more divinely aligned thinking, Steve arrived and remarked that all our tomato plants seemed to have inexplicably grown about eighteen inches taller overnight. On closer inspection I noticed they also appeared to be laden with more than twice as many full-size tomatoes as the day before.

After my second day of divinely aligned cauliflower spraying, the same tomato plants were now heaving with still more clusters of beautiful plump tomatoes. All told, our tomato harvest would now be more than triple the original yields.

In my experience, the knock-on effect of seeing more like the Creator sees, brings all kinds of exponential, unlooked-for miracles seemingly out of left field. This was no exception. Thanks to this higher-frequency timeline, not only did my cauliflowers thrive, but we would now be enjoying homemade tomato pasta sauce all throughout the following year.

Which brings us to powerful point Number Two: Maybe this is how the world gets healed of its many gaping wounds. Maybe this is how climate change is reversed. It seems to me this lesson can be scaled up to include the world's most seemingly intractable issues. If we can take responsibility for the quality of our own thoughts, mindfully aligning them with divinity instead, every time we catch ourselves pointing fingers at the enemies who got us into this mess—who knows.

Maybe that action alone would be enough to pop us into incrementally cleaner and healthier timelines. Dimensional possibilities where ocean plastic, or air pollution, or fracking has never been a thing. Or at least, far less of a thing. And can you imagine what other unexpectedly beautiful delights of Nature might also exist in that somewhat-higher frequency timeline?

Or let's take it even one step farther. Imagine, if you will, dozens of people picking up trash on a beach (appropriate action) all the while carefully seeing both the trash and those who discarded it as divinely holy expressions of our shared Source (appropriate perception). Imagine the potential ripple effects created by this mindfully intentional combo platter of divine alignment. Who knows what lovely, life-affirming timelines the planet might shift into, if such high-frequency behavior became commonplace among us?

Do you doubt it's possible? It's impossible only if you say it is. You're a multi-dimensional spark of God-flame, kiddo. You can do it. We all can.

THREE

Butterflies and window washers

With my reconfigured navigation system up and running, the spiritual journey it inspired unfolded slowly and gently, in ways that at first seemed very unspectacular and mundane. Nothing felt like dramatic progress, initially. I spent the first few months simply teaching myself the new discipline of unrelenting kindness, as I learned to embrace the subterranean self with compassion in every moment, no matter how it was behaving—and no matter what mood I was in.

The effects of this practice seemed cumulative. Under the benevolent gaze of the divine self within, the subterranean ego self slowly blossomed and became willing to actively participate, sharing its deepest unconscious secrets as needed. In this always-gentle process, the unlikely trio of divine self, submerged iceberg and I, cooperated on what ultimately became a grand adventure of liberation.

Everything about this evolutionary journey has felt quite different from the agreed-upon collective ideas about the awakening process. The usual metaphor for the spiritual awakening process is the caterpillar's transformation into a butterfly. The caterpillar lives his wiggly little existence for as long as necessary, then cocoons himself to kick off the transformation.

Once inside, he swiftly breaks down into an unrecognizable pulp. In this demolition process nothing of the caterpillar himself remains. And the be-winged end product, the splendidly awakened divine self who no longer eats your prize geraniums, is seen as being so much more wonderful than the lowly caterpillar, the inconvenient personal 'me' self from whence it emerged.

The comparison is understandable. It contains big nuggets of truth. But do you notice the underlying current of self-hatred running through it? It takes for granted the ordinary egoic self is the unwanted obstacle to awakening. It assumes the inconvenient old self must be got rid of pronto, so the shinier, newer divine self can emerge.

The implication is that it takes nothing more than a heroic act of will to let go of the inferior old self. Never mind that few seem able to accomplish this act of will in actual practice. I certainly couldn't. This personal failing, this inability to let go of ourselves is seen as the only thing standing between us and our experience of divinity.

The good-riddance-to-bad-rubbish implication is, this magnificent, newly emergent divine self (if we ever manage to become it) will fly away without so much as a backward glance at its own shredded egoic cocoon.

I dunno. I can only go by my own experience. To me, the awakening process is more like walking around my own house's perimeter and performing a gentle window washing, day after day. Gradually the Light is let in. When the outside panes have become somewhat clearer, I then choose to knock on the door and ask permission to wash them from the inside too.

Oh so slowly, the once-filthy panes of glass become more and more transparent to the Light that's always been here. And after enough Light has been allowed to enter, a type of quiet transmutation starts to occur.

This soft alchemy is no magic trick of transformation. It does not suddenly make an unwanted obstacle disappear, revealing a marvelous new butterfly-ish 'me' in its place. As it finally occurs to me that everything, honest-to-God, really is God,

I begin to patiently wash my own windows with greatest tenderness and respect.

Not to remove the unsightly crud, but simply as an expression of care and devotion. I am, after all, God washing the God off of God. I'm not judging the dirt or the windows. Why would I? That would be silly. I'm just practicing attentive self-care. It doesn't even matter, ultimately, whether stuck on bits of grimy gunk are coming off or not. Holiness is.

Take a look around, inside and outside your own life. Maybe it's not what you imagined it would turn out to be. Washing the God off of God is a practice of genuinely learning not to mind what's here right now. And that acceptance, in itself, is a form of mastery leading to a type of enlightenment.

When washing the God off of God is our genuine window-washing attitude, the interior of our house grows rapidly brighter. And as the interior illuminates, *the house itself and all its contents* start to wake up and recognize themselves as the same Light that's been softly streaming in all along.

And that's the alchemy. Inner crud slowly remembers itself as divinity, which inspires the aforementioned crud to accept Light instead of resisting it. The more Light it embraces, the easier it is for the crud to more fully recognize its own identity as God.

(Won't that make the crud arrogant, believing itself to be God? Uh, no. The crud has spent its whole self-hating existence believing in its profound unworthiness. The recognition of its own divinity, which is not a belief but rather a direct knowing, causes it to realize, for the very first time, that it has an authentic right to be. Along with every other part of all-that-is.)

The cleaning of one's own muddy windows is an oversimplified analogy describing this gradual evolution toward inner union. In actual practice the process of window washing is neither linear nor straightforward. Although higher and lower selves are ultimately one, and the decision to treat both with love and respect is profound, their aims are not the same.

The higher divine self desires only our freedom and eternal happiness. The worldly subterranean self will do whatever it can to keep the game alive. Both are innocent; one of them just doesn't know it. As my relationship with the subterranean self deepened, I naturally wanted to ease its suffering. If it was asking for mercy, my instinct was to offer it. Yet in my experience one reaches key points again and again in the journey, where allegiance to Light must clearly be chosen.

The subterranean self benefits greatly from increased Light streaming in through its partly cleaned windows. It feels happier and so do we. Yet this submerged self needs at least a minimal amount of crud on its windows in order to survive. As long as it survives, both we and our subterranean self will remain in bondage together. For its sake and ours, therefore, divine Love will inspire us to choose against the subterranean self's pleas for indefinitely protracted survival.

This isn't tough love. It's the opposite of tough, and the opposite of small 'l' love. The tenderest divine Love imaginable is what inspires us to hold the subterranean self close to our hearts, in the authentic desire to spare it further unhappiness.

Love and compassion for all parts of the self, will help us bring the higher and lower selves together holistically. In my experience an attitude of love and compassion is a definite must if we want to experience true spiritual alchemy—the kind where nothing ever needs to be killed off or abandoned, in order for the magnificent awakened self to emerge and take flight.

The body's role in awakening

Over the decades grace offered me more than one awakening opportunity I'd seemingly said yes to. At least, the top ten percent of the iceberg said yes. But sometimes in more recent years, a much larger percentage—maybe even a majority percentage of the self appeared to have said yes as well. Or so I thought. Yet I never seemed able to hold onto any of these awakenings for more than a few days at most.

As it turned out, this body, bless its heart, wasn't structurally ready to handle all that divine Light. Part of the human body's job description is to accept every uncomfortable memory or traumatic belief we don't feel able to deal with on a conscious level. Even stuff we don't know about.

With grave determination and steadfast loyalty, the body stores all this un-decomposed gunk inside its own energy field, and within the physical cells. So to some degree, it doesn't even matter if our conscious mind is interested in awakening. Our unconscious stuff hidden deep in the physical body and energy field is busy doing its own robustly oblivious thing—and what it's doing is the opposite of what's required for awakening.

So let's say grace smiles upon us, and we experience a transcendent moment of spiritual Light, eternal bliss and divine unconditional Love. Our energy field (which includes the body, of course; it's just the slowest, densest portion of our field) is flooded with recognition of the magnificent Love-Light-Awareness that's always here in truth.

Yet if our energy field is chock full of old unresolved stuff, and our cells are filled to the brim with lower frequency, unconscious beliefs about our self and our world, there is no room for that flood of high frequency Light to find a permanent home. If our cells are unable to let go of old unconscious stuff, they can't make enough room in which to digest and metabolize high frequency Light.

As one who unknowingly spent years pushing vast quantities of spiritual Light at myself in hopes of profound transformation, I can tell you this: If the cells can't metabolize it, the Light will have nowhere to go. It will spark around and around in your system in highly uncomfortable ways, short circuiting until it eventually burns itself out. No harm done, it's just not pleasant or helpful.

Various techniques exist for clearing and opening the cells, to help them make room to metabolize ever-greater amounts of Light. These range from emotional processing of the old stored traumatic gunk; to mysticism and spiritual alchemy; to release of stuck energy through breathwork; and even to purely nutritional means.

(Purely nutritional means: There are those who are convinced spiritual enlightenment comes as an inevitable byproduct of nutritionally healthy cell function. When super-healthy cells are correctly doing their thing, they can metabolize maximum amounts of high frequency Light. Therefore, the theory goes, if we strive to make our cells super-healthy, we'll be so Light-filled that embodied awakening will just sort of happen all by itself. I'd love it if that were true. And who knows, maybe it is. It has not, however, been my experience, nor that of anybody I know.)

In any case, whatever methods you choose to employ, I heart-ily recommend making some room in your cells for greater amounts of spiritual Light to dwell there. I recommend it even if your spiritual path of choice might not seem, at first glance, to support that direction.

Many excellent spiritual teachings say the body is not real, and that is certainly true. The only thing that's real and true is Love-Light-Awareness, or Source, or God-Creator, or what-ever the heck you want to call it. Or if you want to be even more excruciatingly accurate, we would ultimately look past creation and creatorship altogether, to the formless Absolute. The Absolute is the only unchanging reality. Creation, which includes bodies, qualifies only as illusory *stuff*. Y'know, for gaming purposes.

Be that as it may. I know the body isn't real. You know the body isn't real. But the body itself has no fricken idea it isn't real. It may therefore require some patient help to get up to speed on that bit of news. Until it does, it will obliviously and effectively deflect all our attempts to metabolize more spiritual

Light. And (unless it turns out they're right about that nutrition business) there won't be a damn thing we can do about it.

I speak from long experience. I came into this world with a profound desire to not come into this world. I didn't want to be in a body. That's not a unique attitude; lots of shy or empathic or artistic or spiritual or introverted or sensitive people feel much the same. They're born, they take one look around and say, 'Oh, HELL no.'

And the rest of their lives are spent tiptoeing around grudgingly, barely present inside their own skin. I was one of those. When I finally turned to spiritual practices, naturally I gravitated to one that denied the body's reality. *The body is an illusion, you say? Excellent!* I couldn't wait to shed that shit, and cavort as pristine spirit instead. And now I had the best possible excuse.

Yet bypassing the body never works. Even though it seems (to some of us) to be merely an unwelcome tag-along we never meant to invite to the divinity party. We're simply not going anyplace without it.

When the body is perceived as an unsafe enemy, or a shadowy bucket of shame and trauma, we cannot and will not leave it behind. In my experience, an absolute prerequisite for lasting peace is the willingness to surrender completely into being here, which includes being in the body.

If you're an athlete entirely comfortable with your own physicality, being in the body may not sound like a big deal. But if you've never tried it, you may be surprised to discover just how challenging a practice it can be, to sit quietly for any length of time in presence, inside your own body.

If you recall, this is where all our old undigested gunk is stored, and to be present in the body means we've stopped running away from everything that's been warehoused here. We don't get to bypass our stuff, on the way to transcendent peace. We don't have to nitpick and analyze it, but we do have to sit still willingly and agree to be present with it in the Light of Awareness.

No matter what it looks like or how it behaves, the body and its storehouse of stuff is worthy of Love and acceptance.

The Fricken Map is Upside Down

Maybe even heartfelt gratitude, too, for its decades of unsung effort. Slowly, eventually, the body becomes recognized as a cherished friend. And at that point, we find the physical self is no longer an obstacle to awakening, because we're not trying to escape from it anymore.

A few years ago, I was still pretty heavily into hatred and resistance toward my own body. I hated how it looked and acted. Various body parts and certain bodily functions still held deep shame. I was consciously aware by then none of this was actually the body's fault.

I wanted to feel genuine gratitude for my body, knowing it didn't deserve the unrelenting abuse I heaped upon it. I longed to be able to look at myself in the mirror and not criticize what I saw there. For years I'd been working with self-love and self-acceptance in meditation, yet the fiercely critical inner judge wasn't even slightly impressed by my efforts.

Back then I still perceived the wisdom of the higher self as coming in from somewhere other than my own core essence. One morning, fresh out of the shower and full of dissatisfaction with my shameful physicality, I received an unusually frank message from my higher self about the body's true nature. Here is an excerpt:

Your body is perfect. Your body is an indivisible part of a perfect system of creation, which was intentionally chosen by you, and by all of humanity.

At the inception of the soul, each human is gifted with a vertical column of Light originating from divine Source. It is part of the non-physical aspect of the human body. The Light runs vertically up the center of the physical body structure.

This stream of Light is constantly with you, it is yours. It contains the full knowledge of your own individual aspect of divinity, your own true identity, and all the Love that heaven holds for you. You couldn't lose it if you tried—and you have indeed tried very hard.

Your body is also gifted with a system of energy centers, each one vibrating at its own unique frequency. Everything in your world, your universe, is composed of energy in motion. The body is no exception. Everything is vibration, operating at various frequencies from very low to very high.

Unconditional Love is a vibrational frequency—a very high one. If you want to embody the state of unconditional Love (and you say you do) it is merely a matter of raising your own energetic frequencies high enough to be compatible with it.

You have been asking, 'What holds me back from fully embodying the state of unconditional Love? What holds me back from releasing the personal self and choosing divinity as my true expression on this plane?'

This is what holds you back. The body is a vehicle of divinity. It was always designed to be. Yes, in your experience it has uncomfortable urges, inconvenient needs. It shits, it farts. It ages and breaks down in various ways. It demands sexual or other forms of gratification. Even so. The body is an intrinsic part of the package. It is your divine vehicle. Your gateway.

Humanity has overlaid a complex system of collective agreements onto the body: The body is dirty. Its requirements of elimination are shameful. Menstrual blood, which is nothing more than the neutral shedding of the uterine lining, is taboo in virtually every culture.

And then there are the agreed upon ideals of physical beauty and youthful appearance, and the immense pain of self-abnegation that comes with falling short of those ideals.

Shame and hatred for your own physical vehicle are deeply woven into the human psyche—and therefore into the cells of the body as well as the vibratory field you emit. If you could only see the divine magnificence of the body's true energetic potential, you would clearly recognize the enormity of your error.

The Light of heaven can only be metabolized and brought to Earth by a body that has been wholly forgiven by the self. A body that is cherished and recognized as a sacred part of all-that-is. Even though its shit may continue to stink. Even though it may sprout gray hairs in increasingly unlikely places.

World religions and cultures have promoted the idea of body shame and hatred, in part as a way of keeping you from discovering your own divinity. Make no mistake. There is no more surefire way of blocking full expression of the divine AS you, than by refusing to witness the body in the truth of its perfection. The physical body is the wholly neutral gateway to heaven on Earth. To lock the gate and bar the door is to simply never experience that holy union.

(Yes, my higher self occasionally swore like a sailor on shore leave, because that was sometimes the best way to get through to me.) At the time, this lesson about bodies, frequencies and divine energetic potential was received as shocking new information. Nowadays my own ongoing experience with it testifies to its undeniable accuracy.

Here is one other important aspect of the body's role within awakening consciousness: In much the same way that the body will not be bypassed even though it isn't real, the world itself (totally ultra-not-real as well!) can't be bypassed either. The world and everything in it, including our own body, must be loved and embraced, welcomed and forgiven. Only after we forgive it and accept its present-moment imperfect-perfection, will its illusory nature become clear to us. Only then can we begin to truly see like the Creator sees, thereby transcending the world.

But here's the funny thing: Even when when we're looking past the illusion, to see like the Creator sees, the world's illusory nature still won't inspire us to ignore it or dismiss it or bypass it. Anything but. Yes, we do transcend the world, but that's because everywhere in the world we look, we recognize heaven on Earth. Even though the world may still be behaving as it always has. And that recognition of the world's inherent holiness might very well inspire us to take helpful action. Or, perhaps more accurately, to *be* helpful action.

Gandhi said it, and it's one of the world's most brilliant, bumper-sticker-friendly spiritual quotes of all time. *Be the change you wish to see in the world.* The quote is deservedly famous. It points directly toward infinite transcendent wisdom, yet still manages to offer practical advice no matter what our level of consciousness might happen to be right now. It meets us where we're at. And then when our own consciousness deepens, we discover the quote does too. Levels upon levels of meaning, all pointing directly toward truth.

On the surface, *Be the change you wish to see in the world* is simple and obvious. It means if you hate seeing litter in the park, go be the one to clean it up. (And it's okay if you silently bitch to yourself about the messy habits of others while you're doing it. At least you're inspired to take action. You're helping to make your neighborhood a tidier place for all to enjoy.)

The next deeper level of meaning would be, for example, if you want to see more peace in the world, alter your own personal behavior and attitude in order to plant the seeds of peace. Help your neighbors—yes maybe even those same messy ones who litter in the park. And then take it further. Be patient and respectful with those of differing opinions. Prioritize cooperation in all you do, rather than competition or conflict.

The next deeper level after that carries an exponentially greater degree of personal commitment: If you want a peaceful world, think peaceful thoughts. This one is harder. Because, as we know, peaceful thoughts are not usually the subterranean self's preferred form of expression. Not all the time, anyway, because we're bumping up against the distinctly un-peaceful thoughts of others (as well as our own) all day long.

It would take a Herculean amount of self-mastery to remain at peace within the mosh pit of collective human expression. Yet the aspirational decision not to participate in this collective tumult, is a profound one. Thoughts, like everything else in existence, are vibratory in nature. They matter. They *create* matter. To only contribute thought-forms of peaceful intent, therefore, would be a wonderful gift to the planet, indeed.

Yet even that isn't as deep as the rabbit hole goes. This, to me, is the true and final meaning of *Be the change*: If you want to see a more peaceful world, *be* peace itself. Embody peace until peace is your sole identity. You will then, quite naturally, be a beacon of true peace, radiating it to all others. And because you are its radiant epicenter, a peaceful world emanates from your very being.

This is how key the body's role is, in both the awakening process and the type of world service one might be inspired to perform on behalf of all beings. The clue is in the word: Embodiment. Em-body-ment. It is only when the Light of divinity is embodied—metabolized by (and therefore as) the body—that your divine self can start to show up as you.

When Light is embodied, peace can start to walk around as you. You emanate the vibratory signature of peace itself, which carries the divine potential to influence the entire collective for the greater good of all. Therefore, your contribution to world peace is exponentially greater than it could otherwise be.

Gandhi embodied peace. He was also a social activist. Hence his suggestion that if we want to engage in some seriously powerful activism, we should take inspired action to pick up the litter and help our neighbor too. Engage in all the levels of *Be the change*. But for maximum impact, do it from the standpoint of embodied peace. When we do, he suggests, we'll see for ourselves how radically and powerfully our illusory world changes to reflect us.

It doesn't just have to be peace, of course. The world is sorely in need of just about any higher-vibration state you can think of. *I choose to be kindness. I choose to be self-forgiveness. I choose to be the infinite recognition that cauliflower-loving bugs are divine beings in truth.* Our inner radiance of whatever embodied state we choose, is what gets powerfully transmitted to all. It doesn't fit on a bumper sticker, but that's okay.

Tell me where it hurts

Bodies, man. Can't live with 'em, but just try living without 'em. As one whose physicality has been no stranger to discomfort, I've had plenty of opportunity over the decades to perceive both the body and its malfunctioning behavior as enemies. Yet neither one is quite what it appears to be. More recently I've come to recognize pain, as well as the body housing it, as wise gurus and steadfast friends.

Pain and the suffering that accompanies it, are two separate things. We tend to experience *painandsuffering* as all one sensation lumped seamlessly together. But as it turns out, the suffering is an optional add-on, entirely due to the influence of the subterranean self. It's fascinating to feel just how different the experience of pain can be, when it occurs outside the subterranean self's identity structures.

And herein lies another clue about the deeply unhelpful nature of the subterranean operating system itself. As we've already noted, the subterranean aspects of the self are responsible for weaving a personal identity for us, more or less out of thin air. The weaving of a personal identity out of millions of individual data points seems a harmless enough activity. It isn't.

Besides sending us down the wrong roads toward faulty conclusions (as in my LA freeway example), this process of automatically categorizing and linking the things we perceive now with historical precedents and future imaginings, turns out to be the very activity that indirectly creates all our mental and physical suffering.

All our seemingly innocuous personal data points collectively form the distorted lens through which we can't help but compare and resist, criticize and judge ourselves and our world. The data points themselves obstruct all hope of experiencing true peace.

The gurus have been telling us this truth all along, of course. The so-called ego *is* the source of all suffering. That's an unavoidable part of its job description. It's the knock-on effect of building a personal self that can't help but function to resist and block out the peace of God. But I maintain there are no evil-geniussy criminal motivations behind its doings. The illusory frequency the subterranean self emits simply jams the God broadcast, that's all.

Back to pain without suffering: It's an odd sensation. The first time I experienced physical pain minus suffering was back in 2013, during yet another of those brief awakening events. On this occasion I'd had an encounter with Thich Nhat Hanh, an enlightened master, in a vision the night before.

In the vision I was standing fifty feet away from him in a stark concrete courtyard. He turned to look at me, and as our eyes met, his piercing gaze transmitted a palpable vibratory wave of enlightened realization deep into my mind. I felt the powerful, high-frequency wave shudder awkwardly through my energy field, and I lost my physical balance.

As I was falling sideways onto the concrete I realized I had a choice. I could put out my hands in an attempt to break my fall, which I knew would severely limit the power of this awakening transmission. Or I could surrender to the powerful vibratory wave and let myself fall unimpeded, even if it meant my head might smash open like a pumpkin on the concrete. I chose the pumpkin option. The vision ended just before my head hit the ground.

I arose from my bed the next morning to find an entirely silent inner state of being. Gone was the usual mental chatter. It was a typical September day in Southern California, cloudlessly sunny and warm, so I dressed in jeans and a sleeveless tank top and drove to the beach. It seemed as good a place as any to get used to the unfamiliar inner quiet. This wasn't transcendent peace I was feeling, exactly, nevertheless the egoic self was nowhere to be found. All inner turmoil had ceased.

I parked the car and made my way toward the water. Nobody was around, so I sat down on the sand and tried meditating. It was a nice, effortlessly spacious feeling. But within a minute or two the wind picked up so strongly, hurling the sand with such unexpected force that it was starting to sandblast my skin. Weird, the weather had seemed so calm a minute ago. I opened my eyes to investigate.

Directly in front of me, the blackest clouds I'd ever seen had gathered in ominous billowing layers to obscure the horizon. Beneath them the turbulent sea had turned a brilliant emerald green, frothed with whitecaps. I was startled to feel icy rage emitted by that water, and understood immediately that the scene in front of me was a physical out-picturing of my own intense internal resistance to permanent awakening.

I tuned in deep within, and noticed for the first time a faint and faraway rumble of dissent coming from the region of my abandoned mine. As I focused in on it more closely I felt the unruly ruckus of unconscious resistance that was still present somewhere within me, hiding beneath a vast blanket of pristine silence. No wonder this inner state hadn't quite felt like transcendent peace.

Back in 2013 I was still a little bit enamored of my own drama, and true to form, I couldn't help but marvel at the ferocious beauty of sea and sky I was witnessing. I found its unbridled fury mesmerizing. But I couldn't linger to admire it for very long. The temperature was dropping and the wind was rapidly picking up speed, the sand striking my bare skin with ever-greater force.

I stood up to go find a café across the road where I could enjoy shelter and a cappuccino. It was then I realized the horizon in all other directions had remained cloudless, sunny and presumably warm. I was in my own tiny, bitterly cold and unforgiving micro-climate.

Walking slowly through the marina, I watched calmly as the yachts bumped and rocked madly in their slips. The wind shrieked an earsplitting dirge, the boats' metal riggings whining eerily as they clanged and scraped against hollow metal masts. Both my ears ached from the cold and the deafening cacophony; the ear facing the ocean was also being pummeled relentlessly with frozen sand at full force. It was extremely painful.

That's when I noticed the genuinely odd sensation of pain minus suffering. It's kind of like pain doesn't hurt. Or rather, it does hurt, but it's irrelevant. It couldn't possibly affect your inner state, which is entirely untouched by the

The Fricken Map is Upside Down

discomfort. In no way would pain ruin your day, no matter how intense it might be.

That mini-awakening lasted a bit longer than most of the others. But after a few days the angry inner foot-dragger reasserted its supremacy. And for a long while afterward the experience of pain without suffering remained a mere memory, a curious side benefit of a short-term, partial awakening.

*　　*　　*　　*

Several months ago I was experimenting, just for fun, with deep surrender into knowing the divinity of a painful condition—with no agenda other than recognizing its perfect identity. If everything is God, I figured, this must be too. So I was trying to feel into that knowing, as fully as I could. Because why not? Pain was here. I might as well occupy myself with the game of unmasking its true identity. I held the pain in steady recognition of its pure divinity. And not unlike that peculiar sandblasted hunt for a cappuccino back in 2013, I discovered the pain was present yet it didn't hurt. Or, it hurt, but it wasn't bothersome in any way.

These more recent explorations into the nature of pain went deeper than they did back in 2013. This time I noticed it was a beautiful expression of radiant divinity. I marveled at the wondrous gift this pain revealed itself to be. I was honored by its presence. And because it was already perfect right here, right now, its choice of whether to stay or go was of no importance at all.

(As it happened, the pain chose to leave after a day or two of being recognized as divinity. The mysterious condition, which showed up all of a sudden, disappeared without a trace as quickly as it had arrived. But I didn't require that outcome. Or any outcome.)

Although we've talked mainly about physical pain here, the same would surely hold true for mental-emotional pain. The good news is, whatever form of inner or outer discomfort we're experiencing, pain without suffering can be known prior to permanent embodied awakening. All it takes to explore the sensation of pain without suffering is an attitude of gentle curiosity, an open mind, and an abiding trust relationship with the subterranean self.

In my experience, when we reach the point that we value this self almost as much as we value the divine Light of our own perfect Source, the subterranean self will gladly do everything in its power to help us taste spiritual freedom. Out of loyalty. Out of gratitude. Out of relief to no longer be the object of persecution.

It will back away as much as it dares, intentionally limiting its own influence, so we can experience miraculous glimpses of the transcendent self we truly are. It hopes we'll be satisfied with these glimpses. It hopes we'll stop short of choosing a different operating system altogether.

The subterranean self can't help being what it is. It is keenly aware its very existence brings a world of suffering to itself and you in equal measure. And yet it knows no other way to be. There is no other way it *can* be.

Despite what the subterranean self would prefer, please don't be satisfied with mere miraculous glimpses of yourself. Dive into the infinite beauty of your own true divine identity. You'll never regret the unfolding mystery and adventure of discovering who and what you really are.

And as for the subterranean self—although it may not seem like it now, ultimately no greater gift can be given it, than peace and liberation from its own dilemma at last.

The Fricken Map is Upside Down

The fungus among us

For more than a year I'd been repeatedly asking for clarification on how to see, or deal with, inner and outer enemies. (I wasn't locked in battle with anybody in particular; the ever-present energetic frequencies of attack and defense in my self and my world had themselves simply become too painful to endure.)

In response to those requests, various puzzle pieces had been slowly dropping into place, like the lettuce, housefly and cauliflower insights I mentioned earlier. As a result I was gradually learning to step away from my own lens of perception in order to see more clearly.

Last summer I asked yet again in meditation what more I needed to know, about how to correctly perceive this business of enemies and transgression. In response I was shown an image of strong netting, its helter-skelter strands densely woven in some areas, other areas more loosely structured. In an accompanying rush of divine information I understood the netting symbolized the core foundation on which this personal identity rested: A foundation of enemy consciousness.

A personal self can't sustain the illusion of being separate from all that is, unless its core foundation is built upon the opposite of Love and Light. Loosely translated, this means belief in enemies. As much as I'd been trying to hold the opposite intention, looking back I recognized now, I had always seen those transgressive garden bugs from within the all-pervasive context of enemies.

I'd been attempting to pluck the transgressors out of the fabric of my enemy consciousness and lift them higher, where they alone could be viewed through a clearer lens. Yet the fabric from which they came remained as adversarial as it had always been. As I gazed at this impressively constructed net, I realized nothing about my self or world had ever truly been perceived in any other way, despite my many meditation exercise attempts.

A divinely inspired question now arose within: *Am I truly willing to release my belief in enemies?* The subterranean self held its breath to see what my answer would be. Enemy consciousness, after all, was a non-negotiable prerequisite for its very existence.

I paused to appreciate once again the raw deal the subterranean self had signed up for: The constant insecurity of never knowing where the next enemy will turn up, forever unable to feel truly safe. Yet its only other option was oblivion, the result of returning to its Source. What a choice.

Awash in bittersweet gratitude, I turned toward the subterranean self. *'We deserve to let ourselves off the hook. We deserve to know peace.'* Holding all parts of the self in quiet love and admiration, I felt it relax. It agreed not to resist.

October 3, 2018

Now it's a few months later, and this time I felt a completely different knowing arise, when I was once again shown the image of the same strong netting. I was originally shown it back in July, to symbolize the thought system that supports enemy consciousness. Back then, I was still mainly seeing the world through that pervasive enemy lens. The strong netting was a perfect visual symbol for it; I could feel the all-encompassing adversarial worldview of that netting firsthand, throughout my mind, body and field. It was kind of shocking at the time, to recognize just how pervasive the enemy thought system really is.

This time, when prompted to revisit the image of the strong net, I didn't see it in the context of enemies. In the intervening months two things have changed. I've been experimenting more seriously with exploring life from outside the lens of enemy consciousness. I've also been researching how to farm organic mushrooms.

Hence this time I instantly recognized the netting for what it really was: A beneficial fungal network. What I'd been shown back in July was actually the vast mycelial support system running just beneath the surface of an old-growth forest. This is the system nature relies upon to bring nourishment to all trees living there. Without this cooperative fungal network, a forest wouldn't thrive.

Three months ago this helter-skelter netting radiated enemy consciousness. This time it emanated helpfulness born of pristine neutrality. I clearly felt its soft divinity as my own.

Afterward I was blown away to realize I'd viewed the identical image in two radically different contexts, supporting two entirely opposing viewpoints. Both meanings had been accurate. Both had been appropriate to the lens I'd been perceiving through at the time. Wow. So...is perception ever trustworthy? Um. Good question.

Here's the good answer to that good question: It's only the subterranean lens of perception that can't be trusted for accuracy. To see more like the Creator sees (as in my second, divinity-assisted viewing of the same image) is not really seeing through a perceptual lens at all. It's timeless truth recognizing itself, in all it witnesses.

To step outside the faulty perceptual lens of the personal self, we're required to release our attachment to the facts we think we know about an enemy—because facts aren't terribly good at helping us accurately evaluate any enemy anywhere.

Oh, we'll want to believe the facts. We're hardwired for it. But to rise up high enough to witness the truth that awaits us beyond enemy perception, we are required to admit there's only so far the facts can take us. Truth and facts are not bedfellows. Truth is true, and facts are endlessly malleable data point perceptions. They are unstable structures of opinion, perceived a little differently by each of us on any given day. And as I discovered, they're entirely dependent on the lens we're viewing them through at the time.

The wise spiritual adept therefore learns to put the facts aside, in order to see a given situation more clearly. Without facts to cloud our view, everything we see just *is*. And when anything is witnessed as it is—just being, just existing, with no ironclad historical references wrapped around it—the truth of its divinity has the opportunity to shine through.

Oddly enough, even the egoic thought system of enemy consciousness itself is completely neutral. It is not the enemy and never was. It just looks like an enemy, because its very presence is a lens that obscures true vision. And when that view is turned upon itself, it—we—can't help but perceive an enemy lurking within.

When we look at the world or ourselves and assign judgments of good and bad, or degrees of worth and unworthiness, this itself is proof we're seeing through the murky lens of enemy consciousness. We can't not. The countless individual data points we use to form judgments, are themselves fundamental to this egoic perceptual lens. Judgment and enemy consciousness are ultimately the same thing.

Bottom line: As long as we assume our own perception of anything is the correct viewpoint, it's impossible to see correctly. Only when every judgment (good or bad) is set aside, can accurate vision begin to emerge.

FOUR

No such thing as a roadblock

The following experience of learning to surmount a key road-block, signaled the start of my accelerated liberation. Of course it didn't seem that way at the time; in many ways, life was still lumping along as it always had. In fact, everything had been quietly changing at a fundamental level over the previous six months or so. And very soon these cumulative changes would burst forth in stunning new ways.

I'm sure you know what I'm talking about, when I refer to roadblocks: One of your old sticky patterns arises in front of your face *again*, just like it's being doing all your life. You've hit this wall so many times before; nothing you've ever tried has successfully released you from its grip. It seems like nothing ever will.

It's those damn data points again—they make every obstacle seem far bigger and realer than it actually is. But no matter what the illusory obstacle may be, a solution exists for it in truth. With the recognition that God-Creator-Source is infinitely powerful (and nothing else besides God-Creator-Source exists in truth), lifelong roadblocks start to evaporate with ease.

This aspirational recognition of divine omnipotence—I call it 'calculated delusionality'—has been a major influence upon my journey in recent times. This decision for God's solo power was the tipping point that allowed the unfolding of all that has occurred for me.

Calculated delusionality is my response to this critical choice point conundrum: Before we honestly know from personal experience that God-Creator-Source is the only true power, we will need to consciously choose to believe it. This calculated decision feels delusional while we're making it. It feels unsupported by fact. (Once chosen, it soon becomes an authentic knowing, at least during meditation, if not in daily life.)

To me this decision for delusionality feels quite different from blind faith. Nor is it quite the same thing as 'fake it 'til you make it.' This is more of a smart, targeted gamble. It's a clear-eyed choice to risk being wildly wrong on this particular topic. We are putting all our precious pearls into this invisible basket, so to speak, in full recognition that our faith in the existence of the basket itself might be completely misplaced. But we realize we can't carry our unwieldy armload of treasures even one step farther without it.

We're learning to override the fierce inner skeptic who wants to see and feel personal proof of God's omnipotence before it takes the risk of allowing belief to flourish. But that will never happen. Self-protective skepticism exists on a frequency level too low for divine omnipotence to be felt and experienced firsthand.

As I discovered, it's an important attitudinal bridge to cross. If God-Creator-Source is the only power in this present moment, then no matter how stuck or tangled our most persistent patterns are, or how formidable the roadblocks to freedom may seem, they have no power when viewed this way.

I'll give you an example. The following was one of my earliest experiences with calculated delusionality, and the resulting release of a lifelong roadblock.

My life was shaped by two major roadblocks. This was one of them: I came into this world in a flurry of life-and-death drama. Due to childbirth complications, my mother lay on her deathbed. My father was told to choose between her life and mine, as the doctors deemed only one of us would make it through the birthing process alive. Naturally, he chose his wife.

I was aware of this devastating decision as it was being made. Through the prenatal eyes of the infant I was at the time, I understood I'd shown up to keep my end of the bargain, but I wasn't good enough to make the cut. I would therefore be cast out and left to die.

I didn't die, of course. Nevertheless, I believed I had been abandoned first by God, who clearly didn't give a shit, and then by my parents who apparently didn't either. And who could blame any of them? They knew best. Obviously something about me wasn't right.

This ingrained belief in abandonment, betrayal and my own fundamentally defective core essence formed the primary unconscious lens through which I would go on to view life. As a preemptive measure, I closed my wounded infant heart and built strong, icy defenses against further pain and rejection.

Much of my spiritual work over the years had therefore been focused on opening the frozen heart and neutralizing its heavily armored defenses. One small problem: Many well-armed aspects of this subterranean self saw protection against an open heart as their primary function in life. They were acting as loyal guardians and foot soldiers, in an authentic desire to be supremely helpful. In their view they were assuring our mutual survival.

For many years I saw this fortified heart as my ultimate roadblock. I would seem to be making progress in delving into these regions of inner hurt, but just when real vulnerability seemed possible, unknown aspects of the self would slam shut any openings I might've created.

For a while I mistakenly regarded these aspects of the self as my enemies. It took me a long time to realize they were bravely trying to do their bit, not only against external threat, but also against the near constant attack I was conducting in my quest to dismantle these careful defenses.

In meditation one day last summer as I rested inside this heart area, I was overcome by a spontaneous rush of love and gratitude for these determined sentinels, who had been work-

The Fricken Map is Upside Down

ing so diligently for so many years to protect the heart from harm. In this rush of heartfelt gratitude I felt a layer of defense unexpectedly drop away.

I found myself in an inner sanctum I'd never been able to access before. I explored this hushed and hallowed ground for a moment, feeling so honored at last to be granted witness. And then I saw it: A grenade buried deep inside the heart.

These mysterious guardians of the self had shown me dire warning images before. Their purpose was always to caution me I'd stumbled upon a dangerous roadblock and must not venture farther. For many years I bought into it, nervously backing off, alarmed by such stark imagery.

But over the past couple of years I'd gradually stopped playing along, no longer scared off by warnings. Had I been shown the grenade image during that period, I wouldn't have even paused. Given my unrelenting determination to befriend all parts of the self, I would've marched right up to that scary grenade, intending to pull the ring and find out what it was made of. But before I could've reached it, the startled self would undoubtedly have reacted by shrouding the image in mist, never letting it be witnessed again. No meant no. I would not be allowed past that point.

Ultimately, whether I obeyed a warning image or courageously tried to move beyond it, the discouraging result was always the same. So, yeah. For most of my life I fully believed in the existence of roadblocks.

This time it was different. I saw the grenade. I paused respectfully. In a great *whoosh* of inner recognition, I realized for the first time that all aspects of the self have extremely good reasons for everything they do. It had never occurred to me this might be so; I had always believed they resisted simply because 'that's what subterranean selves do.'

In fact, all aspects of the self are courageously intelligent. They are utterly committed to our mutual survival. From their own points of view, their beliefs and behaviors are the correct ones and should always be given full respect. (From my point of view it looked a little different. But never mind. This wasn't about me.)

So with all this in mind, I neither approached the grenade nor did I turn away from it. Instead I turned my focus to the one who issued the warning, and gave it my unstinting love and admiration. I treated it as an equal. I thanked it respectfully for its loyalty and hard work, and then ended the meditation.

Later on, after resting in meditation for a few minutes I knew what to do next. I went back to the grenade, and chose to recognize both the grenade and the heart surrounding it were equally made of God, exactly as they were right now. The grenade didn't need to become anything other than what it was. It was God expressing as a grenade. It was already perfect.

I held this meditative focus for several minutes until I truly believed it; I felt the grenade's soft holiness, and therefore my own. Next I made the delusional choice to disregard an entire lifetime of heavily armored roadblocks, and focus only on God's omnipotence in this moment. As I held this radiant focus, I saw and felt the irrelevance and powerlessness of the heavy armor.

I could now see inside the grenade, and to my surprise the interior was empty spaciousness. Or to be more precise, it was filled with God to the same degree as the heart surrounding it. Nothing was here that could stop me. How can God prevent God from entering God? More to the point, why would it want to? *Whoosh*, a gentle shift wafted in on the breeze of this recognition.

Within about forty-eight hours, brand new kinds of thoughts started popping up in my consciousness as I made my way through the day. Loving thoughts. Grateful thoughts. Thoughts that could risk leading to an open heart.

My attitude toward my own physicality shifted the most dramatically. I'd always been unrelentingly judgmental toward the physical self—I just wasn't my type, you know? I was critical of my looks, my posture, my aging body and its health limitations. Although decades of earnest work had softened the tone of this caustic self-talk, the underlying judge who inspired it had never vacated its post in the slightest. Until now.

I first noticed this attitudinal shift when chronic foot pain made itself known, as it has periodically throughout my life. A couple of mornings after that meditation, as I arose from bed my feet complained bitterly about taking my weight. This occasionally happens for a few crippling seconds, while the feet grow accustomed once again to the tiresome requirements of gravity. Usually I would've noticed the pain and automatically lamented its presence.

But this time, unexpectedly, I went straight into open-hearted gratitude, thanking my feet for all they have endured over the years. I marveled at their ability to handle sixty years of non-functioning arches, and still take me hiking. *Dudes. You are awesome. Thank you.* This was such a new thought-form, I was instantly taken aback.

Yet gratitude seemed to have become much more my default position, whenever my body complained. Achy back from too much gardening? *Oh spine. You make it possible for me to do so much.* It was as if the pain itself had become just another opportunity to appreciate this unsung physicality for all it did on my behalf.

One day later that week in my morning meditation, I was resting as the sacred Light of Awareness inside this newly available heart space. A sudden divinely inspired insight bubbled up out of the silence: *I am prior to all wounds and defenses.*

I was here first, in other words. The consciousness that I am, was already present before any baggage was added on. The prenatal wounds and defenses (no matter how well-armored or deeply entrenched they may have been) were clearly not my core identity. They were not an intrinsic part of me; that would've been impossible. *Whoosh.* Another layer of crusty old heart armor peeled away, replaced by yet more divine Light.

It's true of everyone, of course. We're all pure, unfettered divinity. And our divine identity is prior to all virtual reality games. Prior to all push-me-pull-you magnetic polarities of light/dark; good/bad; or abundance/lack. Our heavily defended fortifications and ingrained responses to threat are not who we are.

A few days after that I was watching a bird in flight, and out of nowhere a startling proposition suddenly arose from the depths: *I could drop all defenses and Love that bird with my whole heart.* Such a strange idea had never occurred before. Yet I could see it had merit. This would be a perfect beginner relationship for a delicate, newly awakening divine heart. The encounter would be holy, yet fleeting and anonymous, with no risk of rejection.

I gave my heart permission to try. And in that moment, I realized it's always been within my power to make this choice. I just didn't know it. I'd been banging on the door of my own heart for most of my life. How funny that the key had been hidden inside my own closed fist.

And so, as the unsuspecting bird winged its way toward the horizon, I took the supreme risk of opening to Love it. Although I could tell portions of my heart were still somewhat numb or fuzzy, I was overjoyed to discover that opening up to un-defended divine Love was no longer a hopeless pipe dream. I found I was neither locked out of my own armored heart, nor imprisoned in its numbed-out frozen depths.

This is why I say with great certainty there is no such thing as a roadblock, in truth. As we begin to see more like our Creator sees, we open to infinite new worlds of possibility. New forms of wisdom. New solutions to every conceivable problem. We become able, maybe for the very first time, to look down and notice the key resting quietly in our own beautiful palm.

Spiritual alchemy and emotional processing

What happened with my heart is a small example of a powerful phenomenon called spiritual alchemy. In case this book is your first introduction to it, we'll pause for a description. The word 'alchemy,' as it's used here, does not refer to an arcane art. This isn't magic. Spiritual alchemy is described in this way because it brings about transmutation.

Trans-*formation* means to alter the existing self. Trans-*mutation* is true metamorphosis. Emotional processing (in which we seek to heal one individual wound after another, in hopes of attaining emotional freedom) is a process of gradual transformation.

✗   Spiritual alchemy (which transcends the entire wounded playing field at once) is experienced as metamorphosis of the self. It's a process of coming to recognize one's own true nature as a divine being, which in turn inspires profound change within the mind-body-energy field of the one who engages with it. And this is why calculated delusionality is such an important complementary practice. Recognition of God's solo omnipotence is a requirement for spiritual alchemy.

In working with the omnipotent Love-Light of divine Awareness, our pain and limitation are transmuted. Or that's how we experience it, anyway. It would probably be more accurate to say we are simply lifted higher than the frequencies where the wounds, pain or limitations can affect us.

I suppose you could say this book, while offering deep respect to both kinds of work, is really an ode to the virtues of spiritual alchemy. Besides the fact it's so much faster, smoother and exponentially more powerful, I believe there's another important reason to place more overall trust in spiritual alchemy than in emotional processing.

✗   The subterranean self, once it gets used to the intimacy of emotional processing, will encourage us to keep at it pretty much forever. Thanks to its multi-dimensional, multi-lifetime playing field, we will never experience a shortage of stuff to process.

Carrie Triffet

This highly engrossing partnership of discovery and healing will serve to keep the subterranean self alive and functioning indefinitely. It's easy for us to get caught up in the whole fascinating healing process. But if we do, the result will probably not be what we're hoping for.

I'm fairly certain there's no such thing as attaining spiritual and emotional freedom 'once we've reached the end of our processing.' That would be sort of like Googling one set of search terms continuously, and avidly studying every page of results, hoping, by doing so, to reach the end of the internet. ✷ And yet. If you're somebody with past life traumas—or even this life traumas—those painful patterns will be running behind the scenes as strongly magnetic autopilot programs, almost certainly blocking all your attempts to move straight into spiritual alchemy. Some amount of emotional processing will likely be necessary, just to gain enough spacious clarity to be able to move into the rarefied realm of spiritual alchemy. Emotional processing is therefore an indispensable tool for any intrepid spiritual explorer.

Those sticky autopilot programs go on running unchecked until they are met with our fearless compassion, gratitude and acceptance. Personally I've found emotional processing a worthy and irreplaceable part of the spiritual journey. Not only does it open the way to alchemy, it helps teach us unconditional love and acceptance of our own subterranean self. And therefore the subterranean selves of others.

*   *   *   *

I had despaired for so many years about the unreachable nature of my own heart. I longed to experience the truth of divine Love, yet processing alone could never bridge that seemingly insurmountable gap. With spiritual alchemy (and calculated delusionality) I simply began to rest as the divine Love I already am, to the best of my ability, in the inner heart space. Even though I only felt Love's resonance dimly at first, I knew the heart itself was being softly energized and awakened out of its long, painful slumber by this truth.

The Fricken Map is Upside Down

Inner wisdom had inspired me to rest in this way for several days in a row, in morning meditation. Each day I could feel the heart space becoming more and more energized with this resonance of divine Love. The more the heart space powered up, the more clearly I could feel the barriers and chronic deficiencies of this forever work-in-progress heart melting into irrelevance.

These very real obstructions and barriers were not denied in any way. Alchemy is the opposite of denial. I didn't try to leap over the barriers and wounds in order to get to the Light of Love. That would qualify as spiritual bypassing, which is what happens when we still unconsciously believe in the power and purpose of such barriers. Because we believe in them, we're still subject to their strongly sticky magnetic pull. Eventually that magnetic pull will prove to be stronger than our upward leaping momentum, which is why spiritual bypassing is never successful for long.

Spiritual alchemy means belief has been withdrawn from the powerful barriers themselves, and transferred instead to the true power of the limitless Source within. And from that higher wisdom standpoint it is clearly recognized that, although on one level these lifelong barriers and obstructions are very real and always have been, they are in truth powerless and meaningless. There is no point to their expression. And so their time is up.

By siding with Source we've chosen something other than outdated allegiance to limitation and pain. We're resting as divine Love itself, so we can't help but be loving and compassionate as we witness this obsolete set of creaky structures that used to seem so imposing. And as we recognize these irrelevant old roadblocks and barriers are no longer what we want or need, they are 'bypassed' in a true way. A permanent way.

This happens, as I said earlier, because our own vibratory frequency has lifted us into a closer alignment with our Source. We're genuinely seeing more like the Creator sees, which means our frequency has moved higher than the level where such self-limiting beliefs and structures can affect us. And so they no longer do.

A closer look at hotbuttons

One last puzzle piece from the updated worldview remains to be discussed before we move on. It's about the processes I now use for dealing with the subterranean self's hotbuttons, both in meditation and in daily life. With the divine self always in charge of the journey, these hotbutton mastery processes have helped me excavate the subterranean 'mine' at last.

Because hotbuttons residing in the submerged iceberg are wired directly to the conscious personality self, some type of mindfulness practice is needed to interrupt the inevitable knee-jerk response that happens every time a button gets pressed. There are different ways to go about this. We can use emotional processing to directly face the issue the hotbutton represents. This dismantles the button itself, so no matter how hard it's pressed, we don't get triggered.

Another type of hotbutton mastery is to become increasingly comfortable in our power as the witness. We consciously notice we've been triggered; instead of reacting, we immediately take our attention inward to the one who's been triggered, not to the outer circumstance that pressed the button, or even to the button itself. We thank the one who's been triggered. This aspect of the self is doing us a great service, by showing us where our internal unhealed wounds are calling for our attention.

Choosing not to react outwardly is, at this stage of the game, a conscious decision. We recognize the trigger itself is meaningless—even though our mind may be shouting all the reasons the trigger deserves to be attacked. The specific thing that triggered us may seem to urgently deserve our knee-jerk response, but in truth any old trigger of a similar nature would do. This one is not so special. Something within us needs to blow off steam by activating that particular hotbutton. But why? Who is it that needs to release inner steam through outward attack?

The internal one is our focus. We are the patiently curious witness, as we offer it our compassionate, non-judging attention. We're not here to fix it, or its hotbuttons. We sit with it quietly in the Light of Awareness. We ask permission to feel

The Fricken Map is Upside Down

what it feels, so it no longer has to carry its burdens alone. This method of hotbutton mastery is a blend of spiritual alchemy and emotional processing. As with all spiritual alchemy, the divine Light of Awareness is firmly in charge. It alone does the work.

Of the two methods for attaining hotbutton mastery outlined above, in my experience a combo works best. We dismantle the buttons that allow it; these are usually the simpler, more straightforward ones. And in the case of deeper or more tangled up patterns, first we patiently allow the knotted bundle of strings to be detangled on our behalf. Our higher self does this work for us; our job is simply to witness the knots in the Light of Awareness. This divine detangling process will help us see where the hotbutton actually resides, at which point we can choose to follow it inward instead of reacting outward, and sit with the one who blows off steam.

A third form of mastery can also work wonders with certain types of hotbuttons. It involves retraining our brain by simply refusing to react, on any level, to a hotbutton that gets pressed. This is about rewiring the brain to make different neural connections. An emotional response to any given trigger releases corresponding chemicals in the brain. We tend to get unconsciously hooked on those chemicals. By not responding to an emotional trigger, we deny the brain its fix.

If we can keep it up long enough, different neural pathways are formed, and the habit of getting triggered by a given hotbutton may be replaced by the habit of not getting triggered by it. At which point the (unexamined) button dismantles itself, because it no longer serves its intended purpose. Although simpler, this is a somewhat more advanced form of mastery. And again, it may or may not be as effective in cases where the hotbuttons seem too tangled or complex.

In general, our mastery efforts are bad news for the subterranean self, or at least for those wounded or armored energy aspects it seeks to protect on our behalf. Of the three methods for hotbutton mastery, the subterranean self would much prefer we work with types one and two, which allow it to guide our inner journey through the iceberg's hotbuttons. This way it can keep itself and its progeny alive for as long as possible.

(Not that there's anything evil about that desire. This inner aspect of your self is made entirely out of you. Don't you yourself prefer to survive? Why would another part of you feel any differently?)

? But this is why a policy of keeping the divine Light of Awareness firmly in charge of exploration is a must. Although the innocent desire to survive may be entirely understandable, it's still not a great idea to encourage the subterranean self to linger indefinitely. Its aims and goals of keeping you safe no matter what are contrary to your own best interests and wellbeing.

I'll share with you some divine wisdom that filtered in last year, on this topic of hotbuttons and the subterranean self's natural tendency toward self-preservation. I woke up one morning on the very wrong side of the bed for no particular reason. Disgruntled with life in general, I lay there inventing an imaginary conflict scenario with somebody I hadn't seen in years, bitterly telling him off for something he hadn't done and was never likely to do in the future. Yikes.

To wake up in the morning already sunk deep into this kind of abrasive worldview was mercifully rare for me. I was caught off guard by its ugly tone, surprised that such a grating nose-dive would occur during a period that had been so otherwise infused with ever-more radiant divine Light.

I despaired a little bit as I got out of bed, at the apparently unlimited regenerative power reserves of my much-diminished subterranean self. Like a cranky phoenix, rising again and again from its own embittered ashes. With a sigh I responded to this depressing thought the way I'd long since trained myself to do: I gave it my love and gratitude. And my heartfelt respect. And then I got up and began my day.

Apparently in answer to my despair at the never-ending power of my own subterranean self, my morning meditation began abruptly with a clear image of what used to be my ninety percent iceberg. It was no longer submerged. Half melted,

The Fricken Map is Upside Down

this comparatively smallish mountain glowed soft white, lit from within by the Light of divine Awareness. At least a dozen random hotspots could be seen in various places on the mountain's surface, burning with a fiercer light than the surrounding areas. Some of them winked out as new ones lit up elsewhere, giving the illuminated mountain a sort of beguiling firefly impression.

I understood the divine message conveyed by this image: To chase after the hotspots themselves, alluring as they may be, is indeed an endless activity. The subterranean self has a virtually limitless multi-dimensional storehouse of them to draw upon. Furthermore, if that's where I place my greatest focus, the self will naturally conclude I must really enjoy this sort of fascinating journey of discovery. It will work overtime to helpfully present as many opportunities for hotbutton exploration as it can.

Divine wisdom continued to bubble up from within: If a particular hotspot is crying out for my attention, by all means I should explore it with all the love and compassion I can. I should give it my deepest respect. It is calling for a reason. Its appearance is an invitation to defuse, once and for all, the self-limiting belief it represents. But the mountain itself does not diminish in size through the hunting down of hotbuttons. Mine had reduced by half and become lit from within, I was given to realize, through divinely alchemical means.

Just then, the glowing white slipcover was whisked off my mountain, revealing the craggy mound was actually made of a huge pile of gold sovereigns. *This is what all icebergs are made of,* inner wisdom informed me, *and the mountain's true nature is revealed as soon as the fear of divine Love is voluntarily released.*

I understood it was the word 'sovereign' that was important here, more than the image of the gold coins. This wasn't an abundance lesson—although limitless abundance is certainly one of the attributes implicit in the acceptance of infinite divine Love as our own identity. This mountain of coins was about something else. The message here was saying, *contrary to the*

Carrie Triffet

mistakenly limited ideas I have always believed about myself, I am actually a huge pile of rich sovereignty.

I am not at the mercy of any hotbutton—which, after all, is nothing more than a sticky set of obstinate energetic or mental-emotional patterns. I am not at the mercy of an ill-tempered phoenix. I am not at the mercy of anything. I am sovereign, and what I say goes. And in that meditation moment at least, I knew it was true.

The most terrifying thing is to accept oneself completely.
~ Carl Jung

FIVE

What's lost is found

I mentioned two major roadblocks earlier, that have defined my life since birth. As I've said, the unavailable heart was one of them. Yet I didn't start to truly despair over the state of my heart until relatively late in life. Until after I'd already begun my first spiritual practice.

The following essays tell of the other roadblock. The one that had my full attention from the moment I was born, never diminishing in power or importance for the next sixty years: Terror of the supernatural.

I'd spent most of my life trying to find ways to manage the terror—or later, through spiritual practices, to cure it somehow. In response to these efforts, the bone-chilling dread simply moved deeper underground. Impossible to get at, yet hard to ignore.

It was only after I began working sincerely in partnership with all parts of the self, through a combination of emotional processing and spiritual alchemy, that long-held unconscious secrets began to unravel and reveal themselves in ways so magnificent, so gentle and so divinely timed, it astonishes me still.

This series of breakthrough events happened mainly within the past year, but the story leading up to all this begins earlier. April of 2012, to be exact.

Ancient secrets – part one

Some years ago on a visit to Southern England, I took a trip with friends to see the legendary town of Glastonbury. My friends wanted to tour the ruins of the famous abbey, so I tagged along.

Glastonbury Abbey is a lovely spot, its ruined monastery now a beautifully presented museum complete with gift shop. Manicured lawns are dotted with picturesque remnants of imposingly grand stone window arches. These ruins are all that's left of what had once been a thriving, powerful and supremely wealthy seat of the Christian church.

Yet Glastonbury's appeal goes way deeper than its Christian history. A legendary spiritual center dating as far back as 5,000 BC, one of Glastonbury's several alternate names is Avalon, linking it firmly to Arthurian legend. The abbey itself lays dubious historical claim to being the home of King Arthur and Guinevere's grave site.

Various sites scattered around Glastonbury have long been considered sacred to Druids and Wiccans, as well as early Christians including Joseph of Aramathea—and maybe the two Marys too, if you believe the European legends. Many stories claim the holy family made its way by boat to Southern France after the crucifixion, and eventually migrated to Southwest England. Various legends place Jesus at Glastonbury too, although they can't seem to agree whether he visited as a young boy, or as an adult post-Resurrection.

Today the whole town drips with magic, along with overlapping Arthurian myths and legends of early Christianity. Unsurprisingly it is a powerful draw for pagans, mystics and New Age believers of all kinds, as well as visitors from all over the world who come for reasons of spiritual, religious and/or historical pilgrimage.

Besides its long history as a site of pilgrimage, this area has an equally long history of violence and suppression. Over the centuries, each victorious group of invaders bloodily subdued the ones who came before, only to be themselves overpowered by the next wave of conquerors.

Glastonbury Abbey survived in various forms throughout this turbulent history, only to meet its final end in the Sixteenth Century when it was destroyed along with many other Catholic monasteries, by order of Henry VIII. Its abbot was found guilty of treason and hanged atop the sacred Tor for all to witness. After the hanging, his body was torn to bits in the gruesome custom of the day, his head left to rot on a pike at the entrance to his ransacked monastery.

I bring all this up to give you a little background as I found myself, on that rainy, overcast day in April of 2012, sitting alone on a park bench on the rolling green lawns inside what used to be Glastonbury Abbey. As you might imagine, the place was heaving with unseen energies of all kinds.

April 22, 2012
I can usually tell when ghosts are present, because it feels like they're sitting on my chest, squeezing the air out of my lungs. I don't see them. I'm not that sensitive. (Or if I am, I do a damn good job of blocking it out.) Anyway, an iron lung would've been handy to help me breathe in that place, what with the weight of all those ghostly bricks stacked on my chest.

I don't know why this lifelong terror of the unseen runs so deep. The supernatural world feels like death. Feels like worse

The Fricken Map is Upside Down

than death. *The icy dread is lodged so far down that it's part of my bones, part of my DNA. Twenty-six years of spiritual training would hasten to assure me ghosts are meaningless in their unreality. And that's undoubtedly true in the ultimate scheme of things. But to me, right now? Ghosts are still pretty damn real. And they scare the crap out of me, even the benign ones. And I have no idea why.*

So there I was, sitting alone on that drippy wet bench, sucking air in the unrelenting drizzle. I closed my eyes and was suddenly introduced to an immense, unknown part of me, very ancient and deep-rooted. And this mysteriously ancient part of myself was profoundly connected to all I currently label as 'supernatural.'

Although the familiar cold horror of the supernatural was still present, I also felt an unexpected sense of deep wisdom and infinite peace radiating through me, courtesy of this ancient supernatural self. A spontaneous vow arose out of nowhere and took me completely by surprise, the words flowing out seemingly of their own volition:

'It's time to stop hiding from myself. I will allow in everything I've blocked out. No more resisting, or suppressing, or running away in terror from the supernatural.'

I sat for ages after that, dumbfounded. Trying to grasp what had just happened. Terror of the supernatural has always been with me. I can't even picture who I'd be without it.

And yet I want to make good on that promise. I do. But jeez, it's an awfully big vow. One I can't even pretend I'm able to keep. Not yet, anyway.

*   *   *   *

Laying this supernatural thing to rest had been on my to-do list pretty much since I first drew breath in this world, and it had been very much at the top of that list ever since the earliest days of spiritual practice. Over the years the terror waxed and waned, seeming at times as if it lost steam and had been moved far into the background; other times it would come roaring to life without warning to scare the hell out of me for no particular reason. But even in its quietest moments, the slumbering beast was never completely absent.

I'd long since given up trying to make sense of it. In this life, I'd had approximately zero scuffles with supernatural entities of a dark disposition. The opposite, in fact. All my life I'd walked around under some kind of benevolent bubble, routinely protected from all sorts of things, physical and non-physical. Which in itself, was a beautifully mysterious head-scratcher, since I had no idea who or what was providing that benevolent bubble. I didn't want to know.

I could find no legitimate explanation for this unreasoning terror. Maybe it was some kind of past-life trauma thing. From brief glimpses I'd been shown over the years, it seemed I'd played out the same tragic or terrifying theme over and over in different incarnations. Although the details varied, the key points seemed to remain the same: I was a religious or spiritual figure in a dangerous time of conquest. Each scenario ended badly.

I'd never been all that interested in tracking previous lifetimes. Fascinating though it can be, that kind of in-depth investigation had always struck me as yet another potential distraction; a fun game by the side of the road, ultimately leading nowhere. Yet I'd long suspected some of this traumatic information about other lifetimes must have been precisely what blocked me from knowing true peace in this life. Those inaccessible, abandoned tunnels of mine were undoubtedly full of this scary stuff. Why else would the secrets they held be so insistently guarded?

Over the years I'd tried every way I could think of, to make it clear to both the higher self and the tunnels themselves, that I was willing to be shown any part of this horrifying history that cried out to be seen and released. Despite all efforts at persuasion, I never was permitted to get anywhere near it.

Then within the last couple of years, as I began to cooperate in earnest with both the higher self *and* the subterranean self, an unexpected side effect showed up as a result of this gentle collaboration. I started to notice I wasn't nearly as uneasy in darkened rooms as I'd always been. Intrigued, I started paying closer attention.

The Fricken Map is Upside Down

It's kind of funny, the things that escape notice because they've always been here, hiding in plain sight. The hundreds of tiny moments of dilute fear, the pale anxieties that made up my daily life—so normal, so constant, so well camouflaged as something other than abject terror. They stood out all of a sudden because of their absence. Not just moved to the far background, but for the first time actually missing.

I saw this was precisely because I was now in genuine relationship with a large percentage of my own mind, and this new bond had allowed a portion of the ever-present fearfulness to be released. In this somewhat less fearful inner environment, enough of the traumatized fog had cleared that a startling truth now revealed itself: It had never been outside entities I was afraid of, even though that's the way I'd always experienced it. In truth I'd always been terrified of *me*.

Of me? How was that possible? How could anyone be afraid of themselves? It made no sense. And yet this was exactly what the (by now largely forgotten) Glastonbury vow had suggested. It was time to stop running away from myself. Six years later, it seemed I was ready to begin that process in earnest.

A potent dream I had one night, illustrated this newly emerging relationship with my own 'supernatural' self:

In a garage sale, I'm selling off a pair of very beautiful black velvet evening shoes. I'm selling these elegant shoes because they are too big for me. The potential buyer informs me he can only find one. I head toward my parents' bedroom (!) to search for the other shoe. The door to their room is being held shut by an unseen force.

I pull firmly on the doorknob, until the door reluctantly yields and I step inside the empty room. The door closes by itself. I feel a brief rush of cold fear as I realize the inside doorknob has vanished. There is no way out. (In earlier days this recognition would have induced helpless panic, turning the dream into a nightmare. But not this time.)

A newfound sort of brisk, no-nonsense capability floods through me, and I easily open the door along its edge with my fingers and step out into the hallway. A fluffy orange tabby cat saunters past, and I watch to see if it will confirm that ghosts are indeed holding the door shut, because cats know these things.

As I watch the cat and the door, a sudden whoosh of inner clarity floods my consciousness. I realize the unseen one who holds the door closed is not a ghost at all. It's me. It's always been me. The supernatural of which I've always been so terrified, is nothing more than me sensing my own unknown power. It leaks out into my consciousness, despite my frantic efforts to suppress it.

Standing there in the hallway I make the radical new decision to accept my own mysterious power instead of being scared witless by it. And for the first time ever, I'm suddenly sort of curious to know more about the nature of these potent gifts. I turn toward the cat, who is now lounging on the floor at my feet. I extend my hands toward him, sensing some kind of lovely, benign power will come forth from them. The startled cat looks around as he is harmlessly lifted a foot in the air. And then I wake up.

Ancient secrets – part two

Given my highly dysfunctional lifelong relationship with the unseen world, it's kind of funny that I ended up living here in rural England, not far from Glastonbury itself. Choosing this spot didn't feel intentional at the time.

Maybe it's just me, but the spirit world feels a lot closer here. More ever-present and briskly busy, like it's all around us and it's got important shit to do. I'm not just talking about ghosts, although there are surely plenty of those. Nature spirits, elementals and unseen whatnots of all kinds seem to flourish here on this crowded island on a whole different order of magnitude than they do in highly paved and broadly spacious Southern California.

Supernatural terrors aside, I confess it feels a little strange to be casually chatting with you about the existence of Nature spirits, because A.) I would have thought the whole idea of Nature spirits was ridiculous until just a few years ago. And B.) I'm pretty much the last person you'd expect to be on intimate terms with any part of the natural world. I always lived in moderately urban environments before this, and on those relatively rare occasions I found myself in wilderness, much as I appreciated its beauty, it always made me a little nervous. Too raw. Too survival-of-the-fittest-ish.

All of which made it hugely interesting when last year, Steve and I took on the project of rehabbing an acre of disused land near our home and workshop. The prior long-term tenants on this land had treated it as a dumping ground for all sorts of unholy crap. It held portions of old rusty vehicles, alongside partially un-burned evidence from bonfires so toxic we shuddered to contemplate it.

Most of the ground had been covered in waste nylon carpeting or vinyl sheeting many years earlier in a futile attempt to keep down the weeds. Instead, over the years a thin layer of soil had settled on top of the carpets; by the time we came to take a look at it, the entire field was covered in dead, shoulder-high nettles, brambles and thistles, the neglected field grasses underfoot having formed a thick, spongy layer of rotten, white straw-like mass, home to myriad abandoned rodent nests. The overall vibe of the place was sad, and more than a little bit creepy.

As awful as it was, at the same time other aspects of the property seemed potentially rather good. Being exceptionally fond of privacy away from the prying eyes of the landlord, the previous tenants had planted dense, double rows of fast-growing trees all around the field's perimeter. Fifteen years later, scores of mature hazels, alders, ash and young oaks competed with junipers, five or six species of willow, several elders, a maple, a horse chestnut, some hawthorns, a couple of damson, one particularly sickly crab apple, and a lone copper beech.

All were choked by two or three kinds of invasive vines, climbing merrily over everything in sight, including each other. We could see the potential here. But an acre is a hell of a lot of area to transform, when it's in as sorry a state as this one.

For years we'd been craving an outdoor spot to call our own. Our loft is delightful, we've enjoyed living here. But it has no private spaces around it. No grassy patches or patio areas from which to enjoy the sunset. And we'd been talking more recently about trying our hands at a vegetable garden. And so, after much weighing of pros and cons, that's how we came to take on this ridiculously ambitious project of trying to bring such a badly abused acre as this one back to life.

Gathering advice from experienced farmers around us on how to go about clearing the land, everyone advised hiring a contractor to come in with massive farm equipment to tear up everything but the trees so we could start over. Initially we said no because the land was full of discarded metal, broken crockery, the aforementioned nylon carpeting and all sorts of hidden hazards that would potentially damage the expensive farm equipment, were the driver to unwittingly run over any of it.

But we said no for another reason too. To us, this approach seemed much too brutal. We wanted to clear the dead brush, mainly to uncover whatever had originally been planted fifteen years before it had all become hopelessly overgrown. That meant slow, careful hand work.

All throughout the autumn months Steve and I painstakingly cleared the dead brush, and worked to free as many of

95

the trees from their vine prisons as we could. The spongy matting underfoot proved too much for our mower or strimmer to handle; eventually I took to chopping it by hand, six inches at a time, with hedge clippers. Did I mention how stupidly big an acre is?

We gingerly exposed abandoned rat runs to daylight, and apologized to ants and snails (the only living inhabitants we encountered) as we disturbed their homes. We took away the empty rodent traps and pesticide containers we found buried in the hedge, and brought in bird feeders and compost bins.

And then the winter rains came, turning the place into a floody mess. It was time to stop for the season. We looked around, taking stock. After hundreds of hours of work, the land was still ugly, still brutalized, and as far as we could tell, still dead. We really weren't sure whether or not to continue our efforts in the spring. Should we even bother? It wasn't our land. The owners themselves would find our painstaking efforts eccentric at best. People around here think Prince Charles is crazy for talking to his houseplants. What would they make of our careful efforts to repatriate a baby spider to some other part of the garden?

But then something sort of magical happened that I still can't fully explain. It seemed that Nature itself had noticed and appreciated our efforts to be kind to the smallest bug while tending to the needs of the largest tree: The place did virtually all the rest of the work for us.

Come spring, the matted straw of half a dozen prior neglected summer seasons seemed to melt away on its own, leaving the new spring grasses easily mowable and free to breathe. Trees, shrubs, dog-roses, poppies, lilies, lilacs, iris, honeysuckle and hundreds of showy specimen plants of all kinds burst into joyous bloom. Rows and rows of mature berry bushes, freed of their surrounding overgrowth, suddenly awakened into pure, vibrant vitality.

Treated with neither pesticides nor herbicides, the grassy expanses were soon jostling for space with wildflowers of every kind. Pheasants, grouse, a family of woodpeckers, bats, owls and dozens of other species arrived. The air hummed with moths, butterflies and every kind of bee. Grasshoppers and crickets not seen or heard since Steve's childhood merrily added to the population explosion, along with more creepy-crawlies than you probably need to hear about.

Come early May, the sickly crab apple tree was brimming with health, spilling over with perfect pink blooms, alive with the buzzing of hundreds of bedazzled pollinators. Weeping willows, formerly limp, yellow and disease-ridden, now cloaked themselves in vibrantly healthy velvet foliage hanging majestically to the ground. If you were to walk through this wondrously lush springtime field and choose just one word to describe the vibe it gave off—that word, incredibly and improbably, would be 'Love.'

We'd been inspired by the book *Wilding* that had come out recently, in which thirty-five hundred private acres in Sussex had been left completely unmanaged as an eco experiment, allowing messy, uncontained Nature to behave as it will. It was the only piece of true wilderness in the whole of the UK. The result of this controversial, hands-off approach to the natural world was that all sorts of endangered flora and fauna returned in numbers far beyond anyone's expectation.

Nature, when left entirely to its own devices, quickly found its own balance—and every fungus, animal, weed, bug and beetle played its own crucial role in that balance. This book powerfully influenced my own newly awakening understanding of the innate intelligence at work in the natural world as a whole.

We couldn't do quite the same on our little one-acre parcel, obviously. But at the far end of the property beyond our vegetable beds, greenhouses, wildflower meadows and meandering grassy pathways, the Wilding Experiment inspired us to leave several large, untouched islands of nettle, bramble and thistle, interspersed with a riotous cacophony of other naturally occurring weeds and decomposing detritus.

Each island promptly grew up into a dense, shoulder-high thicket. These thickets provided both food and cover to dozens or maybe even hundreds of species, including one beautiful, large red deer. He graced us with his presence for a few days and nights, stealthily munching on black currants in the early dawn hours before retreating to his secluded thicket for safety.

As someone who had never before felt connected to the natural world, I was beginning to appreciate for the first time its deep wisdom and perfectly orchestrated seasonal rhythms, all from my ringside seat. Around this same time Steve had decided it would be fun to experiment with brewing herbal beers as the monks used to do. So he ordered an American book called *Sacred Healing Herbal Beers*, which I felt inexplicably drawn to read first, even though I'm neither a brewer nor a beer drinker.

I found it enthralling. In it the author traces the history of medicinal and sacred herbs in ancient times (including here in England) and their use in fermented drinks. It's a very thorough book with hundreds of recipes to try, if you happen to live near a hedgerow or field containing wild-flowering endangered herbs all over the place. Which, as it happens, we do.

Reading about all these medicinal plants I had previously thought of only as invasive weeds, was truly an eye opening education. I began to understand all things in Nature have great value to some species or other, even if not always to us. I was especially astonished to find this book spoke of nettles in the most glowing terms imaginable. Nettles! I had no idea they were more or less the perfect food, with just about the full complement of vitamins and minerals, beloved by animals, insects and humans alike.

On the advice of a friend, we made a batch of sun-ripened nettle juice for use as a plant food. Our veg plants vastly preferred it to the store-bought kind. I'd had no experience at all with nettles in Southern California. Here on the land I'd always thought of them only as a painful, stinging nuisance. I apologized to them each time I chopped them down (only to find them regrown twice as robustly a few days later)—but that was because I apologize to anything I chop down.

According to this beer book, nettles make a highly effective tonic for arthritic conditions. Steve's finger joints had been feeling inflamed from overuse lately, so we picked a bucket of nettles (apologizing to them as we did so) and followed one of the book's medicinal recipes for nettle beer. The results, a couple of weeks later, were surprisingly delicious, more like a dry white wine than a beer. Steve and I each poured ourselves half a glass and took a sip. We each immediately felt a slight headache. Hmm. Odd.

We kept sipping anyway, me because it tasted so nice, Steve because he was hoping to alleviate his joint pain. Its effects felt weird. For one thing, I felt very drunk after a couple of sips, even though we'd just eaten a full meal. Steve is an experienced brewer; he'd followed the recipe exactly and was quite sure the alcohol content was no higher than seven percent. That's high for a beer, low for a wine. Yet I felt as if I'd been drinking straight vodka on an empty stomach.

Something else seemed peculiar too. I couldn't put my finger on it. For his part, Steve felt a bit feverish and sick. Neither of us finished our glass. When we went to bed a few hours later, the unsettling effects were still in full force.

I lay down on the bed and turned out the light. The room seemed to spin, but not in an 'I drank too much' sort of way. It felt like a raw force had been unleashed, and was thrashing around inside my consciousness. It felt shamanic, somehow. I observed it, fascinated. Although other wild plants from that herbal beer book are clearly listed as having extra-inebriating, or even psychotropic effects when brewed into beer, nettle is unequivocally not among them. It is listed as a plant that is wholly nurturing and nutritive. The beer is sometimes prescribed as a general tonic for people recovering from serious illness.

I watched as my allegedly nurturing beer crashed around in my consciousness for a while, before becoming gradually aware this potent visitor possessed a consciousness and a deep intelligence of its own. As I tuned into it more closely, I began to realize this unknown representative of the natural world felt very grand, very large, possibly even very regal. Like I was in the presence of the king of the nettles, if there was such a thing. Or maybe it was the king of the Nature spirits.

Whatever it was, it felt extremely powerful. I could tell its attitude toward me was not rage, even though it was raging within me. On the contrary, it seemed curiously loving, almost parental.

It took me awhile to realize I was being admonished—almost the way one might instruct a small child to drop the box of matches NOW. The being informed me I was not permitted to mess around with plant medicine. I had no idea of the power I was playing with.

One should not dabble in the healing arts in this way, it scolded. *Plants are conscious, free-will beings. Respect is required when working with them. Their healing properties are bestowed as gifts, upon those who ask proper permission.*

Chastened, I indicated I understood. I promised not to do it again, and thanked the being for the lesson. Shortly afterward I fell restlessly asleep and, still deeply under the influence, was pulled into a powerful, trance-like dream:

It's a bright, full-moon midnight. I'm outside the red brick Pennsylvania house I grew up in. Unseen voices are engaged in some kind of supernatural ritual somewhere nearby; I don't like it. I'm standing in my childhood backyard, which, curiously, is a tidy English field bordered by hedgerows. I make the conscious decision not to be frightened or upset by the mystical ritual I'm overhearing. For the first time, I'm not going to run away.

I turn back to gaze at the house, where I notice the cellar lights are on. This is the first time in my life the cellar has ever been illuminated, and I realize its profound significance. I know I'll find answers to unconscious secrets there. I want to go in and investigate.

I start to move toward the cellar door, which is shrouded in deep black shadow. As I approach it I hesitate in the inky blackness, unsure, and I wonder: Did I come outside to the backyard through this cellar door? I don't remember doing that. If this isn't the door I came out of, that means it will still be locked from the inside like it always is.

I make my way instead to the front of house (which is a handsome California Craftsman bungalow!) and I see the front door is cracked open, with interior light spilling out. I can hear my ex-husband Kurt in conversation on the phone with someone who I gather is a cherished long-lost relative of mine. He seems to know her. I wonder who on Earth she is, and why would she be calling so late at night?

'How wonderful you'll be arriving soon,' he is saying to her. 'Carrie will be so happy to finally meet you.'

I step inside the house and look at all the stuff Kurt has taken off the bookshelves and piled on the table. In the middle of the books and clutter I zero in on a brightly colored desk globe, pastel countries bordering a pale blue Atlantic Ocean. Startled, I look up at him and ask, 'Are we moving?'

Kurt turns to me and answers firmly, 'You need a way out, and you need a way in.'

I awoke with a start. Still powerfully under the influence, I received an immediate crystal clear vision as a sort of addendum to the dream. I saw my 'house of self,' with a honeycomb warren of rooms stacked vertically atop one another, descending far down into blackness. Each of them held a secret. The knowing arose: I can never force a secret to reveal itself if it doesn't want to. But the choice to *harbor* secrets from myself is mine alone.

I understood. In response I gladly flooded every floor, ceiling and wall of every room in this symbolic house of self, with the divine Love-Light that I am. I sincerely thanked each secret for being, then quietly witnessed the house and all its rooms in the perfect, silent Light of Awareness.

I informed the secrets they were free to stay exactly as they were if they wished—I had no control over that anyway—but I let them know I no longer required them to hold their information out of my consciousness. *I'm not afraid of you anymore*, I told them truthfully, *and I will no longer be a keeper of secrets from myself.*

The next day I woke up unexpectedly refreshed, considering the busy night I'd had. Although all portions of my strange brush with Nature spirits had been valuable indeed, the all-access pass to my house of supernatural secrets had been a gift beyond measure. Although nothing felt different yet, I knew something very powerful had been set in motion by my decision to keep no secrets from myself.

For his part, Steve revealed he'd been sick and feverish all night, but was feeling better now too. Later on he remarked in passing that although he should have been feeling intense discomfort after working with his hands all day, his joints weren't hurting a bit. A parting gift from the nettle king, perhaps? In any case we left that batch of nettle beer alone after that.

A couple of weeks passed. One day in my morning meditation I was prompted to revisit the honeycomb warren that made up my symbolic house of self. Once again, I offered Love and gratitude to each of the secrets housed there, as I held them in the pure Light of Awareness. To my surprise the walls, ceilings and floors of all the rooms spontaneously collapsed like playing cards and melted away. The secrets now had nothing structural holding them in place. They were free to stay or go.

Ancient secrets – part three

One of the side effects of keeping secrets from myself had been the acute recognition of something compulsive within me—something intensely pressurized and unable to relax, lurking way down deep beyond my reach. I was more conscious of it now than I had ever been. I knew the intense pressure itself wasn't growing worse. It was becoming more unbearably evident, simply because I was getting nearer to the core.

Looking back, this intense pressure had been with me ever since my earliest days of spiritual practice, although I wasn't specifically aware of it back then. Muscles and nervous system seemed forever stuck in a default state of high alert. It took me ages to realize many disparate conditions and effects were in fact expressions of this single underlying syndrome.

Insomnia was one part of it. Not realizing the true source of the sleeplessness, for years I tried all kinds of external remedy, the most recent being Epsom salts baths. But, as with every other unsuccessful remedy attempt, I found I was part of the minority for whom the salts' magnesium supplementation created the opposite effect. Instead of calming the nervous system it sent it into a higher state of alert. Because, of course, any attempt to defuse the security alarm was interpreted by the body as a threat.

While food addiction was no longer part of this compulsive syndrome, I could feel the energetic signature of addiction itself still very much present, even though it was no longer permitted to attach itself to food. It had simply been driven deeper underground, in search of other, seemingly less harmful behaviors it could safely latch onto. I gradually came to realize this self had in fact been on high alert since birth, terrified at the prospect of having to exist in a body. It was time for some answers.

A month or so after the 'house of self' experience, I took this high-alert-terror question into my morning meditation. Tuning in deeply, I experienced it as a powerful engine endlessly blowing off steam. Curious now, I asked inwardly what would happen if we didn't constantly blow off the steam? What would happen if we didn't channel the inner pressure into some kind of compulsive behavior? The immediate answer: *Explosion.*

I knew this wasn't actually true. But it was clearly the firm belief of whoever said it. I then tuned in to see if I could locate the one who feared explosion. I was shown a symbolic visual representation that rocked me back on my heels.

June 6, 2018
It was a steam-driven cast iron machine. Industrial revolution-ish, metal arms turning giant flywheels. But this coal-fired monstrosity was only half machine. The upper portion was grafted onto raw living flesh, like some kind of freak steampunk nightmare creature. The human portion on top was an unknown part of the self, a young child in terrible pain. The machine-child emitted one long continuous scream like a hellish factory whistle, as her mechanical parts worked relentlessly to process constant terror.

It's been my observation that each subterranean aspect we encounter chooses the symbolic image of how it wants to show itself, when it first agrees to be seen. If it feels inhuman, it will appear that way. This one, I believe, chose this horrifying industrial image because I was the one who first spoke to it of engines blowing off steam. From this suggestion it cobbled together an identity, to express to me both its own plight and its dreadful function within the depths of my psyche.

I did not flinch or turn away from what it showed me. It was my great honor to witness this ghastly scene; I didn't care who or what was causing its unholy dilemma. I didn't even care whether what I was seeing was symbolic or literal. To be allowed this viewing was a priceless gift of trust. No matter what, I would wholeheartedly embrace this aspect of the self. I would be with it unconditionally, never again leaving it to cope with its terrible burden alone.

I asked permission to come inside the machine. It was granted, willingly. I sat within its engine core for several minutes, simply witnessing it in the gentle Light of Awareness. In response to my conscious attention I could feel things quietly lightening up throughout its mechanical systems.

So much so, that I was next entrusted with a viewing of a small figure, previously hidden. I was allowed to witness the one who rhythmically shoveled the fuel, the red-hot coals of fear, into the machine's boiler. This bit of the self worked steadfastly, head down and concentrating on its grim task, unable to pause for even a moment. It was unconscious to all but its own relentless effort.

I felt into its beliefs, its reason for being. It believed its job was vital. It alone was protecting me by keeping me on high alert. Life was far too dangerous to allow even a moment of true relaxation.

Deep love and gratitude washed through me, in humble acknowledgment of its unsparing loyalty. The divine Light of compassion arose then of its own accord, and flowed through me to engulf the coals, as well as the one holding the shovel.

I felt the heat drain out of them both, as they took on soft, holy Light. I looked past them into the cavernous fear pit where the coals were coming from. I indicated I was willing to feel this fear intimately, because it's a part of the self and therefore a part of God. Instead, Light flowed quietly down into the pit, illuminating and cooling it. I don't know how long I sat there, just letting the fear pit be as it was. All I knew was, it deserved my love too.

Meditation over, I went about my morning. Gradually I noticed I was attending to my usual tasks (folding socks, washing dishes, chopping veg), with more consciously metabolized Light alive and functioning in the deepest subterranean regions than had ever been present before. No longer experienced as an uncomfortable violation, this surplus of divine Light felt welcome and nourishing.

I tuned in and held the machine-child in love and compassion as I worked. It felt easy and natural to do. There was no place I'd rather have been at that moment, than holding this beloved child as my own while doing my daily chores.

Over the next couple of weeks, I periodically felt guided to return to the one who shoveled the coals. I kept being prompted to hold this little guy in the gentle Light of Awareness while he tirelessly saw to his task. I didn't notice any difference in his fixed unconscious behavior during that time, but then I wasn't expecting anything about him to change. I was just holding him in loving witness.

One day as I watched him working, a startling question popped up out of the blue: *What if we switched to a different fuel?* He paused briefly, arm resting on the handle of his shovel as he considered this unheard-of idea.

I waited, intrigued to see what would happen next. He seemed to indicate he was willing to give it a try. In response, the fear pit from which he drew his coals transformed gradually into a column of soft white Light. He dug in, a bit more slowly and tentatively than before, and began deliberately transferring shovelfuls of this precious new fuel, careful not to waste a drop.

June 20, 2018

I can feel ancient stuff breaking open at last. Secrets are shifting and moving in ways I can't quite grasp yet. It's thrilling. I can definitely see the temptation to get fully immersed in this slow-motion unfolding of my hidden secrets. Who are these hitherto unknown parts of the self? What are their backstories? Why do they hurt? How can I rescue them from their pain? And on and on. I see it, but fortunately I'm not buying into it.

The discovery and release of these ancient secrets seems to promise everything I've ever wanted: Liberation. Wholeness. Peace. But somehow I sense this is a carrot being dangled in front of me. My subterranean self, bless its cotton socks, is trying very hard to give me the treasure hunt I seek. And in earlier times, I probably would have taken the bait gladly. But I'm not so easily persuaded these days.

I'm honored to work with every part of the submerged iceberg that shows itself. I bring in the Light of Awareness to witness these unknown aspects of the self and offer them loving acceptance. But thank goodness, I'm also regularly prompted to take the other tack. I dive deep into the silent stillness that I am, leaving behind all stories, all fascinating history, all the inner selves, and everything I think I know about myself.

In the silent Light of Awareness, I simply am. This brings a steady flow of divine wisdom and higher guidance that maintains balance in my inner explorations. It helps me clearly see what's what. It helps me avoid the carrots. And for that I'm very grateful.

*   *   *   *

About my decision to go deep into the core of the subterranean self: By this point I'd been working with all aspects of the self for quite some time. I was only allowed intimate exploration of the machine-child's interior workings at this time because the subterranean self and I had finally reached a point of abiding mutual trust. I had matured. It's not only that I no longer required the keeping of secrets on my behalf. I could finally be trusted not to turn away and reject the secrets themselves, once they decided to come forward. Although they may have considered themselves too ugly or frightening to be witnessed, I no longer did. The subterranean self sensed this, and so I was granted access to this, the first layer of symbolic secrets.

Does everyone harbor secrets like mine? Who knows. Maybe not. Yet every subterranean iceberg definitely harbors hidden things we don't know about—hidden things that are specific to each person's evolutionary trajectory. After all, that's what an iceberg is for.

So whatever you do, never try to force your subterranean self to disclose its hidden secrets prematurely. It isn't kind, and it doesn't work. And please always accept the counsel

The Fricken Map is Upside Down

of your higher self, respecting its wisdom even if you are repeatedly denied access. There is always good reason for this seeming lack of cooperation.

All these parts of the self, higher *and* lower, are privy to the overall state of our psyche, nervous system and cellular body. They know far more than we do. They seek to protect us from our own impatience. What may appear to be an annoying refusal to cooperate is probably the action of the child-self within; chances are it's feeling forced to take the role of parent (and yes, it might be doing it petulantly), because we're not there to do it ourselves. As we mature, these roles slowly reverse. It's been my experience that as this reversal begins to happen, doors open and cooperation blossoms in perfect divine timing.

SIX

In the land of the terminally cranky, all is well

June 27, 2018
For a few days after the young shoveler agreed to switch fuels, I was feeling such newfound clarity of soul purpose. For the first time it felt like I knew exactly why I'm here, what I'm meant to be. It was glorious. And then the subterranean self decided it'd had enough of this brilliantly unobstructed inner clarity, thank you very much.

Not only did I promptly forget what my soul purpose is supposed to be, I fell into a dank, smelly pit of uninspired lethargy. And severely disgruntled to boot. In this recent fit of spacious clarity, I'd been asking for removal of all self-numbing veils. Hooray! Prayer answered. But the answered prayer was not quite what I was expecting.

I hadn't realized the stunning level of pure discontent lurking beneath my surface. My day usually feels remarkably smooth. Things flow, and I rarely get rattled by anything. Other people sometimes mistake my demeanor for inner peace (it's anything but!) yet I've long understood what they mean by it. Thanks to decades of devoted spiritual practice, my day-to-day inner experience of life feels pretty serene and comfortable.

Anxious way down at the core, yes. Unable to fully relax. The serene comfort sits on top of that, like a fluffy blanket. And that's been my version of normal for a very long time. But this. I'd honestly never experienced this degree of grating displeasure at the heart of it all. Now it welled forth like an acid ocean, unmitigated by fluffy blankets, uncaused by any external event.

Ugh. I did my best not to spread it around. I tried to remain a conscious witness; tried to be comfortable in the discomfort. I did my best to be pleasant to others, despite the toxic ooze emanating from my every pore. It was hard to know whether I succeeded or not.

Despite the apparent change of fuel sources, the subterranean operating system was clearly still working overtime to crank out the production of dreadful ick. And without any veils to fuzz the discomfort, let's just say I wasn't having a particularly good week.

Among other things I suddenly became hyper-aware of all the mini-triggers I responded to a hundred times a day. Most of these would've ordinarily escaped my notice, had the numbing veils still been in place. Now they were laid bare, my inner reactions transparently obvious.

As usual I chose not to act on most of these irritants, but now I couldn't help but be aware of each tiny spike of aggravation as it occurred. Funny, because in my own perception, my day was usually experienced as being fairly devoid of triggers. It was those other people around me who were always reacting to triggers. Yeah, right.

After several days in a row of this, I was lying in bed one hot sticky summer night, doing my best to just breathe into the general discomfort. A quiet statement suddenly bubbled up from within: *All is well.*

It was an invitation, a suggestion. *All is well* was offered as a powerful code phrase of divinity. Although it was a gentle and innocent-seeming statement, *All is well* contained within it total purity of divine Light and infinite Love; I understood it as a stand-in phrase meaning God itself. It implied an agreement to release all fear, judgment or dissatisfaction. None of these things could ever coexist with the perfect divine Light I am, the perfect Light that everyone is.

Carrie Triffet

I welcomed *All is well* into every part of my being. Why not? It was the first time all week I'd had any access to the sweetly forgiving Light of divinity. I felt such relief as *All is well* flowed effortlessly into every aspect of my mind, body and energy field.

The subterranean self kicked up an immediate fuss. *'All is well' is a lethal injection!* It whispered, distraught. I was surprised by the vehemence of its reaction to this gently unassuming phrase, but I understood its plight. *All is well* was indeed a devastating blow to the subterranean operating system. I was deeply sympathetic to its dilemma, yet not at all inclined to back off.

This was one of those clear choice points. Do I give in to the wishes of an illusory part of the self (however beautiful and misunderstood it may be)? A part of the self that can only be comfortable if it's expressing some form of pain or discontent? A part of the self that can never know true happiness or peace?

Or do I do the right thing against its wishes, on its behalf? Do I let truth enter, trusting *All is well* to be gentle and respectful as it Lovingly releases this shadow aspect from its own self-made prison?

I chose *All is well*. Beyond its initial objections, the subterranean self could muster no magnetic energy behind its desire to resist. It held no power to impede the flow. I let *All is well* go everywhere within. I let it infuse and rewrite the operating system, with full permission to revise absolutely everything about my self and my world. And then I drifted off to sleep.

In the next morning's meditation I was once again resting as divine Love, as I'd been doing off and on lately. I could detect no inner resistance at all to this meditation, which meant I could go deeper into it than I'd ever managed before. And in the absence of the usual subterranean reluctance, certain truths suddenly became ridiculously self-evident.

Like this one: *Love is one hundred percent appealing.* Weird but true. After having listened to anti-divine Love propaganda whispered from the depths of the iceberg for so many years, it was a peculiar sort of relief to suddenly recognize unbiased truth filtering into my consciousness unimpeded for the first time.

And it kept filtering in: *There are no downsides to full acceptance of divine Love.* This, too, was a brand new truth to somebody who'd subconsciously spent an awfully long time fearing the loss of God knows what, if divine Love were ever to be welcomed fully.

Despite my conscious desire for spiritual awakening, shadowy parts of the subterranean self clearly believed a hostile takeover by divine Love was a fate too awful to contemplate. Thanks to having read *The Power of Now* early in my spiritual journey, the embrace of divine Love had somehow become equated with sitting homeless on a park bench, blissed out and drooling.

Consciously I had stopped fearing the park bench ages ago. *If I'm blissed out and totally at peace,* I reasoned, *who cares if I drool a little? Whatever anybody else thinks, I'll be the one who is completely fine with it.* Yet I had absorbed the fear to a great enough degree that the subterranean self had secretly latched on and run with it.

The fear was not just of the loss of personal identity, although there certainly was that. Loss of income, social approval, relationships; loss of desire to fit in and be normal. Yet now, free from the under-the-radar propaganda campaign, the truth was suddenly revealed in all its no-brainer glory. *Of course* there are no downsides to the full acceptance of divine Love. Why would there be? Divine Love is completely...uh...Loving.

Love, I now realized, *is the answer to everything.* (As if this too was some sort of brilliant original idea, and not the stultifyingly obvious eye-roller it seems.) In a rush of sudden gentle clarity, I realized any problem, any transgression, no matter how grim or unworthy of compassion it may seem, is best handled by first perceiving it through Love's eyes.

Far from leaving one pathetically vulnerable to attack, a hapless, other-cheek-turning doormat, ripe for abuse (as the subterranean self would warn), the act of seeing through Love's eyes is actually what allows transgressors to be perceived clearly. Sized up accurately.

Correct perception of a transgressor automatically opens one up to higher wisdom and clear perception of the situation the transgressor has created—as well as its possible solutions. From there, appropriate action can be taken for the highest wellbeing of all concerned.

That's what my little epiphany was really about. It wasn't so much that divinely aligned perception of so-called enemies is a beneficial thing; the cauliflower eaters had already taught me that one. The real epiphany was that I recognized clearly for the first time, that divine Love is truly a one-size-fits-all remedy. The only one-size-fits-all remedy, in fact.

Opening secrets

Tuning in during morning meditation a few weeks after the shoveler agreed to switch fuels, I once again saw the honeycomb of unsupported secrets floating in their familiar formation without walls, ceilings or floors. I noticed each one of these formerly dark secrets was now illuminated by radiant, soft white divine Light. A sudden heavenly prompt occurred, sort of a 'repeat after me': *I forgive all transgressions against me.* To my great joy, I could feel this statement resonating all the way down into my cellular structure.

And then came another prompt, a little bit stickier than the first one. Okay, a lot stickier: *I forgive myself for transgressing against all others.* I sat with that one very gently, with great patience and care, yet also with clear-eyed, persistently unblinking conscious Awareness. I would not let the statement pass until I could feel it, too, was allowed to be true, resonating deep in the cells of the physical structure.

A few minutes passed in silent stillness. I next saw the young girl who had been part of the unholy machine. Her mechanical bits were gone. She was just a little girl now. I gladly gathered her up into my arms and hugged her, but strangely, she wasn't hugging me back. Although she was alive she seemed curiously lifeless, her head lolling, her arms hanging limp at her sides.

I turned to the young shoveler, of whom I had grown strangely fond, and he, too, seemed drained of life force. I gathered him up as well, and laid both of them carefully and tenderly on the inner altar to God.

I was surprised to be struck then by a sudden wave of inconsolable grief at this loss. They were, after all, illusory aspects of a virtual reality self, and highly inconvenient ones at that. Why would I mourn such things? Besides, I'd been so careful not to get wrapped up in their stories; I didn't get attached. Despite all this, the grief and loss I felt were piercingly real. Brokenhearted, I placed the whole of me upon the altar alongside them, and I cried.

Crowd Source

The next forty-eight hours weren't much fun. I didn't feel right in any part of my being. I wasn't sick, just shivery throughout all mental, physical and energetic systems. I could tell the subterranean self was thrown for a loop by the loss of the machine-child and her fuel tender. It was scrambling madly to patch up the remaining framework in a vain attempt to cope as it always had. But key parts of the foundation had been removed.

Nevertheless I could feel the concentrated effort to create new coping mechanisms, new ways of preserving the status quo. It was time for me to step in and gently take the role of parent. I gathered all parts of the self in close, and held us all lovingly in the divine Light of Awareness. And in that illuminated embrace I forbade any kind of restructuring.

Unsurprisingly, the next day was a lost day. I mostly sat staring at things, feeling uncomfortably near tears. The following morning in meditation, I was prompted to ask once again, as I so often have over the years, to release all belief in enemies. I asked again to see as the Creator sees. In immediate response I was transported.

July 13, 2018
Everything is made of gray stone. Buildings, roads, walls. I'm in a medieval cobblestone town square; it feels like France or England. I can't believe how real this is!

Before me, a crowd of people shouts at me, laughs and jeers, throws things. Their faces are contorted, grotesque. It slowly dawns on me this is a public execution. The mood is bizarrely festive. Some have even brought a picnic to enjoy while they watch me die.

Thankfully, I'm unaware of my body, and I have no idea what state it's in. I have a vague sort of understanding I've been tortured by the authorities for days or weeks leading up to this moment. I don't know what kind of death this is to be. I can't tell whether I wear a hangman's noose, or maybe I'm tied to a stake, the kindling about to be set alight.

As I gaze out on the grimacing faces in front of me, the modern me, the one who sits in meditation realizes I am being offered an opportunity for a do-over. I can relive this experience differently this time. If I want to, I can see this past-life event more like the Creator would see it. I can transcend my belief in enemies.

I'm humbled by this incredible gift of a second chance. And as I say yes to this opportunity to see differently, there's a sort of cinematic moment where the noise stops and I watch them all hoot and gesticulate in silence. Suddenly, spontaneously, I perceive them all as holy beings of perfect, infinite divine Light.

Each one of them emits the most magnificently soft, otherworldly glow, their energy fields demonstrating to me the luminous beings of pure divinity they really are. I feel the exquisite holiness of each one radiate throughout my entire being. I am staggered by their spotless perfection, their eternal beauty. I am awash with joy, rendered speechless by the supreme honor of being in their immaculate presence.

My heart swells and breaks with universal compassion for their terrible plight. In the same moment I've recognized their magnificent Light, I am also made acutely aware of the pain and fear they feel—precisely because they themselves are unable to recognize the holy Light they are. What a tragic fate, to be perfect divine beings but not know it!

Their true identity is so majestic, so glorious, so beloved by their Creator and their creations alike. I keenly feel the aching loss and confusion they feel. I realize they do terrible things only because they don't know who they are.

I'm so grateful in these brief moments I have left, that I can witness them as divine beings on their behalf, since they are not yet capable of doing it for themselves. I would happily go on witnessing their divinity forever if I could. This is my most profound honor, my greatest joy. All else pales by comparison.

And as I behold these holy beings before me, I silently say to them: I know you are the Light of your Source, because I know I am.

And now back to our regularly scheduled programming

As you might surmise, this divine do-over was transformative. Halfway between a supervised tourist attraction sneak-peek of the type mentioned earlier, and an honest-to-God, consciously chosen experience of full-body Christ vision, I'd felt my energy field rearrange itself, at least partway, in response.

A few hours after this heavenly do-over occurred, the luminous knowing of true identity was tested. As often happens, I fell into a discussion of current events with Steve. Left to my own devices, I always tried my best to stay away from news stories of good guys and bad guys. Yet Steve is more actively engaged than I in the news of the world. Bless his beautiful soul, he particularly supports embattled underdogs standing up bravely for peace and justice.

Whenever these topics of good guys and bad guys would surface in our conversation, I would always witness myself and notice I had a choice to abstain. And then I would think, *oh it's okay, I can participate in this discussion. I will stay neutral and not get activated.* And then I would get activated. And I'd be vaguely disappointed in myself afterward for having gone to that place of good guys and bad guys.

It took me years to recognize this good guys/bad guys engagement was yet another subtle form of addiction. I only realized this because I finally noticed it followed the same inner secret dialogue as any other addiction.

I became acutely aware of this secret inner dialogue back when I used to wrestle with food addiction. Of course it wasn't actually a dialogue back then. It was more of a one-sided subconscious whispering campaign: *Food is our safety. It's our only friend.*

As I learned to tune in and become consciously aware of the whispers, I found I was able to question the nonsensical statements as they were made. This conscious scrutiny alone wasn't enough to end the hypnotic, magnetic attachment to the addictive behavior itself, but it signaled the beginning of the end of the larger unconscious pattern. At least as it related to food.

I realized any addictive behavior's intended purpose is always to alleviate pain—even though that's never, ever what actually happens when the addictive behavior is indulged. I was well-practiced at tuning into addictive whisperings by this point, so my secret dialogue about good guys and bad guys had a fairly high degree of consciousness going on in it. As you'll see, I questioned the whispered propaganda more than once, before ultimately being drawn in. The dialogue went something like this:

Me: *I sense a good guys/bad guys discussion starting up. I don't want to engage in this behavior. Whenever I get activated in these conversations about the state of the world, I start judging enemies 'out there.' I never feel good afterward.*

Addiction: *Oh, but this time it's really important that you engage in it. Anyway, don't worry. You can be part of the discussion without getting activated by it.*

Me: *I don't know why I'm taking your word for it. I always get activated. And I'm never happy about it afterward.*

Addiction: *Yes, but this time is different. This particular target of your judgment is not like the others. This one really deserves it.*

Me (eyes glazing over as I get hooked in): *Yes you're absolutely right. This one really deserves it.*

On this day, with the glow from my past-life do-over still radiant within me, Steve handed me a newspaper showcasing a journalist's well-written article about what was wrong with some aspect or other of European politics. As if in slow motion I watched myself respond, sliding down the slope from neutrality into judgment as I always had.

Then I moved back into a brief, illuminated moment of calmly lucid witness, in which I chose not to enthusiastically hold up my end of this conversation. I seriously did not want to judge anybody ever again. I wanted to perceive all enemies as the radiant Light of divinity, now and forever. Because it's awesome. And then a moment later that same curiously magnetic force overtook me once again, and I let it pull me right back in.

Afterward, instead of the usual vague dissatisfaction with myself for having participated, I felt a very clear knowing arise. This magnetic force of enemy addiction had been offered to me by the subterranean self as an escape hatch. It was the self's way of saying, *aww, gee whiz... you don't really mean it, do you?* Like, it was okay for me to insist upon these luminous knowings in visions and meditations, as long as we didn't have to put them into practice in actual life.

In a flash I saw the conscious decision not to engage was an absolutely crucial choice point, one that could only be made in the same moment the temptation to judge arose. It was only in the choice I made there and then in the heat of battle (so to speak!) that true transformation could occur. Until I decided in actual real-time circumstance that I wasn't tempted to see others as anything less than the pure Light of divinity, my magnificent realization of Christ vision would remain no more than a passing exercise.

SEVEN

The C word

As I mentioned, the past life do-over unmistakably fell under the heading of Christ vision. I'll be using the word 'Christ' periodically through the rest of this book, so let's pause for a minute and talk about what is actually meant by that word. Or at least, what I mean when I use that word.

If you go with the dictionary definition, 'Christos' is a Greek word meaning 'anointed.' Religious scholars agree the word is in the same contextual ballpark as 'messiah,' or 'king.' In other words it takes for granted we're talking about Jesus of Nazareth.

That definition presumes there's only one possible Christ, now or ever. But another long-accepted definition of the word 'Christ' is something more akin to what Hindus might define as an Avatar, a divine being appearing in human form. While the advent of an Avatar upon the Earth is recognized as an enormous gift to the world, it isn't understood as a single isolated incident, never to be repeated.

'Christos' obviously isn't the definition we're going with here. 'Avatar,' which also denotes a single, very special incarnated being, isn't either. Our definition is more egalitarian, more everyday-normal than that. Ours is all about Christ consciousness, which is a frequency equally available to all. The Christ, in this definition, is the aspect of divine consciousness that can be embodied in human form.

Here is what that means. Divinity is infinite; the human body-mind-energy field is not. Christ consciousness is the comparatively narrowband slice of the infinite Source spectrum, if you will, that can be metabolized, embodied and known by a living human being.

So we're not talking here about a God-seed born as an extraordinary human baby, exhibiting its divinity from the get-go. We're talking about the potential of any regular, ordinary human being to tune into, and become one with, our shared divine identity.

The Christ is you, in other words, alive and walking around on Earth—minus all your baggage that currently jams the infinite God broadcast already playing within you. The Christ is anybody, at least potentially. In our definition it has nothing at all to do with religion, or who your incredibly awesome Dad is.

According to the above descriptions, Jesus of Nazareth would be considered a Christ-Avatar. He qualifies as both. You and me? Regular garden variety Christs. Potentially, I mean.

We, like everybody else, are composed of Love-Light-Awareness. You and I, potentially, can realize this truth about ourselves. So can anyone. Any human is equally capable of Christhood. To walk as the Christ—or more accurately, for the Christ (a fully immersive divinity generator) to walk as you—just means the complete you, in your entirety, has agreed to this arrangement.

Not just your conscious personality and submerged iceberg. We're talking every bit of you, from your cellular structure to your sympathetic nervous system to your subatomic energy signature. All parts of you would have jointly agreed to be repurposed as a vehicle of high-wattage divinity.

This requirement for total compliance is not due to some perverse heavenly desire to set the bar unattainably high, by the way. It's to make sure you don't fry your circuits.

Mercy me

The past life do-over and subsequent epiphany about judgment were followed by another very bad night, and another wasted day after that. Once again I was rocked by mental, physical and emotional discomfort, this time characterized by powerful waves of divine Light short-circuiting drunkenly throughout my energy body. Tuning in, I was shown an image of the subterranean self, her face badly beaten and lying in a coma. My heart went out to her. Yet I knew I'd be consigning her to an even lengthier stay in hell if I were to back off and stop releasing the hidden secrets.

The following night I received a sudden invitation, quite out of the blue. I was flashed an image. It was one of those paintings of Jesus, pointing to his own radiant heart. I could only see a closeup of the heart and finger, but I knew without a doubt to whom they belonged.

I was being invited to allow the historical figure of Jesus (as opposed to the universal Christ consciousness) into my heart. And before I could even ponder the question of whether I should or shouldn't, I felt something collapse way deep down. Some kind of ancient personal grudge I hadn't even known about, crumbled to dust and my heart was flooded with what I can only describe, in woefully inadequate terms, as 'soft mercy.'

It wasn't Jesus the person who took up residence in my heart (although I was open to that). Apparently I was required to release old secret traumas having to do with Jesus the person, before I could allow in this numinous aspect of the universal Christ that I am. That we all are.

Soft mercy. I wish I could find better words to convey the depth of its tenderness, its sensitivity and divine sweetness, its infinite compassion and acceptance. I'd never felt anything like it before. Balm to my soul, this brand new quality of mercy immediately made its home within my heart. Or more accurately, it merged with the heart itself, becoming one and the same thing.

July 15, 2018

I have offered the bruised and battered subterranean self to this beautifully soft, merciful heart. Who knows, maybe the self has been feeling so beat-up in this process of dissolution precisely because the love being offered until now has lacked divine mercy.

I pray the subterranean self suffers as little as possible, in this inevitable evolutionary process. I have asked this newly emergent bud of the not-yet-blooming merciful heart within, to enfold the subterranean self in its healing balm. I have asked this merciful heart to help it through the difficult process of having its life dismantled. It's the least I can do.

The Fricken Map is Upside Down

A mother's Love

Having briefly witnessed many times (in meditation only) the pure, dynamic magnificence of golden-white Christ Light, it had long been on my spiritual bucket list to know and be an illuminated expression of its limitless sun-like glory. I'd spent the previous few years trying diligently to bring my cells and nervous system up to speed, with an eye toward safely embodying these challenging energies.

Yet more recently, after experiencing inner mercy for the first time, a new sort of illuminated Christ inspiration began filtering into my consciousness. It was a richer expression of these divine energies than I'd previously known.

It was soft in a different way, from any Christ brilliance I'd ever known. Loving in a different way. I was puzzled at first to perceive these changes. From what I could tell, they had little to do with me and my personal journey of evolution. This felt more like a global phenomenon. These changes seemed to be of a newly emerging frequency, and they seemed aimed at humanity as a whole, not just my own previously unreceptive heart.

I couldn't quite put my finger on it. After much thought and a fair amount of meditation on the subject, I fumbled these intuitions into words: There seemed to be something of the divine feminine showing up here.

Being so new to the resonance of my own heart, this information about a divine feminine aspect of the Christ essence felt (to me, anyway) like brand new territory. Maybe others have been experiencing all this for a while now. Maybe it's old news to some. But to me it felt thrillingly new and unheard of.

This more nurturing, more feminine aspect of the Christ was way outside my own field of experience, so I reached out to share it and exchange intel with other intuitive friends. I'd always been more Christ-centric than most of my friends; I worked with these energies daily. In some ways that was great, because I was so familiar with how the Christ resonance feels. Yet in other ways that familiarity made me too close to see the bigger picture. One day, my friend Adele unexpectedly dropped the missing puzzle piece into place, causing a breathtaking new picture to emerge.

After meditating together on these evolving Christ frequencies, we stood and began to stroll through the garden. As we walked I mentioned, in passing, the white-gold nature of the Christ energies as I'd always experienced them: Like a molten sun was asking to make its home in the core of my being.

She stopped and turned to face me. 'Those white-gold energies can burn,' she said. 'They need to be tempered with the divine feminine.'

Suddenly a profound possibility flooded in. We both gasped as the stunning implication hit us: Could it be that the Christ energy as the world has known it, is only half of the whole? We dropped into meditation again, right where we stood, asking to experience the full, true expression of the blended Christ frequencies—the perfect unification of the divine masculine and the divine feminine Christ.

Behind closed eyelids the garden all around us illuminated with soft, exquisite Light, heartbreaking in its delicate beauty. In hushed stillness, the divine feminine and divine masculine Christ energies merged as one and joined with the Earth itself. Unified in this way the Christ felt very different from anything I'd ever experienced before. *Very* different.

Why would these two aspects of the Christ have been perceived as separate energies before now? Your theory is as good as mine. This much I know: The Christ energy as I've known it until recently has always expressed the pure dynamism of its Source. Infinitely perfect and Loving—but so gloriously bright in its golden-white nucleus of molten sunlight that few could ever meet its fiery requirements for physical embodiment. One would pretty much have to be born a Christ-Avatar (or damn close to it), to successfully embody these Source frequencies.

The unified Christ essence that seems to be emerging nowadays is still every bit of that molten perfection, yet with one crucial difference. It now contains the universal divine mother aspects traditionally perceived as belonging to a figure like Mother Mary, or perhaps Quan Yin—the pure essence of feminine mercy. This is infinitely soft, soothing nurturance. It's the eternal compassion of a mother's unconditional Love. She hears your cries. She gets what [you think] your problem is.

This previously segregated aspect of the Christ energy emanates a soothing pink radiance, in marked contrast to the white-gold dynamism that has previously expressed as the embodied Christ essence. Blended together as equals in balanced, unified harmony, the rosy pink of compassionate divine mercy merges with the brilliant sun-like aspect of the Christ frequency.

The resulting fully balanced, masculine-feminine Christ ray (possibly for the first time in human history) now expresses as an infinitely powerful, yet refined and delicate rose-gold frequency of Light. In its soft mercy, this rose-gold ray is somehow able to temper the fiery sun of the Christ essence as we've previously known it. Its reassuring pink-tinged softness helps the challenging Source energies to more easily integrate into the human physical experience.

It's not that this blended Christ expression has never before existed. Those who feel a personal connection with Jesus would surely agree he embodies many of the divine feminine aspects of the Christ, as well as being a full expression of the divine masculine. Many look to Jesus for solace and comfort. He hears their cries.

This change has more to do with humans who seek to embody the Christ energies for ourselves—the garden variety Christ-wannabees. The true significance of this current unification of masculine and feminine Christ frequencies is in its newfound availability to all regular non-Avatars who aspire to Christ embodiment.

Let me spell it out more clearly. In order to permanently embody the dynamic white-gold Light of the Christ, you or I would already have to be pristinely clear and pure inside and out. No misperceptions or shadowy ideas could safely be harbored within our cellular body, mind or energy field, because the dissonance of those lesser frequencies would jar too greatly against the uncompromisingly pure, white-gold frequency of the Christ Light.

We could briefly touch into the magnificent state of Christed Awareness (as I'd been doing lately). But the 'nuclear sun' dynamism of the embodied Christ would be too hard on the nervous system of one whose own frequencies aren't quite up to snuff. Yet the addition of the rosy pink divine feminine Light means we don't have to be nearly so perfect beforehand, in order to safely metabolize the embodied Christ Light. It offers a much more generous window of opportunity, in which to release our lower-frequency beliefs and perceptions.

This combined rosy-golden Light is somehow cooler—or maybe it's simply more reassuring than it was before. We're not scaring the crap out of our own mind, body and energy field by introducing what they would interpret as pure liquid fire into them.

We don't all have to be walking masters anymore, before we can safely surrender our resistance to God, in order to hold the Christ frequencies. Regular people like you and me have an excellent shot at it now, as never before. Thanks to this evenly balanced merging of white-gold and rosy pink frequencies, embodied Christ knowing is now potentially within everyone's reach.

I'm not schooled in esoteric teachings of energy and their corresponding color rays. It isn't my thing. All I can say is, as soon as I began working with these blended aspects of the Christ in my own meditations, I felt the difference instantly.

No longer did the physical cells quail before the overwhelming intensity of white-gold Christ Light. Something about this new blend made the Christ essence infinitely more acceptable. Noticeably more digestible. My body, mind and energy field took in these soft energies of divinity far more willingly and with greatly reduced levels of fear. Even though the rosy-gold unified Christ essence is, if anything, even more powerful, whole and complete than it was before the merger.

The Christ energy is still a fully immersive divinity generator. Yet I was no longer experiencing it as nuclear fusion. I would instead describe the unified rose-gold Christ essence as something like an endlessly potent unfolding of whisper-soft petals; an eternally blooming rose of unimaginable greatness.

That same day, I started a daily meditation practice of sitting as the fully blended, integrated Christ essence, as I am now. Meaning, I rested in knowing the imperfect, unfinished self was fully divine right now. There was nothing to finish, nothing to wait for. And I held this seemingly imperfect self, embracing it softly as the rose-gold Light of the unified Christ I already am in truth.

*   *   *   *

A completely random postscript:
It's a long established practice in both Eastern and Western traditions that spiritual journeyers might sometimes take a new name for themselves somewhere along the road, to express a profound inner shift in identity. I respect the impulse behind it. I've just never personally been drawn to the kinds of esoteric or ethereal names usually chosen to express the new inner radiance.

I have no plans to change my name now or in the future. But if that urge ever were to spontaneously arise, it occurs to me I'd quite like the name 'Rose Gold.'

It's a good, solid, matching-sweater-set of a name, straight out of my parents' suburbia. A secret handshake of a name, redolent of hairspray and Chanel No. Five—yet all the while streaming the eternally unified frequencies of transcendent Christ radiance upon an unsuspecting world.

EIGHT

Getting the message

You will undoubtedly have noticed by now I talk a lot about receiving images and messages from inner wisdom. I also talk about receiving images and messages from the subterranean self. You might be wondering: How do I tell them apart? Mightn't I confuse one with the other sometimes? I used to wonder about that too. I've never been naturally gifted when it comes to psychic communication. The potential for mix-ups seemed alarming at first.

Actually, psychic talent and inner spiritual wisdom are two very different things. Psychic talent is innate. For these naturally gifted people, communication with other planes of existence more or less just happens. Some of these talented individuals go on to hone their natural skills further by undergoing certification training of various kinds. Many professional healers or channelers fall into this category.

Although we, the onlookers, perhaps unfairly tend to assign those highly skilled people all sorts of spiritual authority (whether they want it or not), that isn't automatically appropriate. Inner wisdom is a different bucket of transcendence altogether. Psychically talented people can certainly develop inner wisdom like anybody else, and many do. But it has little to do, in the end, with their natural psychic gifts and abilities.

Anyway, I never had anything I would've described as innate psychic skill. I was sensitive in random and peculiar ways. As a child I regularly experienced what I would now recognize as unstable timelines. Whole city blocks would be missing from the place I had seen them last. Bus schedules seemed to arrange themselves into new configurations every time I looked at them.

At the time I just thought the universe was picking on me, endlessly playing cruel tricks to get me lost for its own amusement. The timelines always settled down into predictable linear patterns whenever I was accompanied by another person. Buses came when they were supposed to. Buildings reliably stayed put. I thought this was because the universe was on its best behavior, not wanting witnesses to its vicious pranks.

Unstable timelines, while unusual in the era of my childhood, seem to show up with ever increasing regularity these days. Nowadays the experience of overlapping or alternating timelines is so common it's been dubbed the 'Mandela Effect.'

The phenomenon was so-named when it was discovered millions of people clearly remembered the worldwide outpouring of grief that occurred when Nelson Mandela died in prison in the 1980s—while many millions of others were equally certain he left prison very much alive, going on to become president of South Africa and winning hundreds of humanitarian awards including the Nobel Peace Prize in the 1990s. (In our current timeline, ex-president Nelson Mandela died in 2013 at the respectable age of ninety-five.)

Anyway. Back when I was a kid, if I had any psychic gifts I definitely didn't want to know about it. Terror of the supernatural meant a blanket rejection of all things unseen. I was no more interested in reaching out to commune with angels than I was with devils. So I squeezed both my physical and non-physical eyes shut, fervently hoping the immaterial world would never get in touch. And for the most part, it never did.

The first clairaudient communiqué I ever heard, at the age of twenty-seven, was the statement, *'Long time no see.'* That sentence, and its accompanying sparkles of playful joy pierced my careful defenses in a way I couldn't ignore. I was mistaken about who or what was doing the talking, but that opening statement led me into a devoted spiritual practice lasting twenty years. Over the course of those two decades the voice spoke only a few times. It was only after the initial awakening in 2005 that I began to hear it more frequently.

By that point I looked forward to the communication, despite its unseen nature. I loved not only the profound wisdom of the voice's observations, but also the kindness it showed me, and the pervasive sense of wellbeing I felt each time it spoke. All of these attributes are key to correctly pinpointing the identity of an unseen communicator, although I didn't know it then.

I had a long way to go before I would learn any of this for myself. Basic skills had to be acquired first. A single phrase of divine wisdom would no longer do; the voice taught me to listen for complete paragraphs, and eventually for long dissertations. Then I learned to speak and ask questions back, for two-way communication. As one spiritual practice made way for the next, over time the voice became my best friend and trusted spiritual teacher.

Early in that second spiritual practice, worried about the possibility of mistaking my own interior voice for this magnificently wise and holy one, I asked the obvious question: 'How do I know it's you talking? (And not the inner evil-genius-tricksy-bastard-saboteur?)'

The answer was perfect for my level of skill and understanding at the time. Basically it said: *Listen for the content. If it's always Loving and helpful, it's coming from me. If it holds any sting of judgment or seeks to limit freedom in any way, it isn't me speaking.* And so I learned discernment. It became my habit to listen carefully to every word, not just for information but for the intention behind it.

By 2009 the voice started asking me to learn a new method of communication. It wanted me to stop hearing in words. It was unlike me to resist a request from the voice, but I balked at that one for at least a year. In releasing the need to hear in words, I was told I would feel as if I'd lost the communication link altogether—but that ultimately communication would not only be restored, I would experience it in a much more direct way.

And that's exactly what happened. I went a year, maybe two, feeling like I'd lost this precious best friend. And then somewhere along the way, the wisdom pipeline began quietly reconstructing itself inside my own interior being. Or that's how it felt, anyway. But now, even though the wisdom itself was divine as ever, I was never sure I could trust it because it seemed to be coming from someplace inside me. How could anything transcendently divine be coming from inside? Holiness is so clean. But in here it was so…icky.

That discomfort sparked the inevitable dark night 'o the soul that occurs when one suddenly realizes nothing is 'out there.' I discovered I was alone in the universe. I *was* the universe. This realization managed to come as a massively rude shock, despite my years of firm intellectual understanding that all is one, and the entire universe is within.

It took a long time to gather the courage to go looking for pristine divinity within. Back then, the subterranean self was bitterly convinced our very existence was defiled beyond redemption. The idea that divinity could exist somewhere inside my unholy self was inconceivable. And yet if it wasn't in here, it wasn't anywhere.

Over the next few years I tried and failed to excavate the subterranean tunnels, attempting to remove those dark, underground beliefs that spoke so firmly of my own terrible inner deficiency. Yet that abandoned mine refused my every attempt. Half-awake and completely alone, I found myself marooned inside an interior universe that didn't even like me. It was an awful place to be.

That's when I dropped my map, and the rest, as they say, is history. The subterranean self eventually agreed to partner with me on the ensuing off-road adventure, even consenting at times to bravely work against its own best interests. Along the way I discovered something quite unexpected. The more transparent this subterranean portion of the self became, the more inner spaciousness I felt. And that meant more room inside to invite divine wisdom to take up permanent residence.

Divine inner wisdom has been in here all along of course, with or without my ability to invite it in. Upon receiving my invitation it didn't arrive from anyplace else. The same is true of you, and of everyone. Your one hundred percent Christed divine self is present right now, just like mine is. It simply waits patiently to be invited, never making a move until it's truly welcome. It waits for you to offer it a spare key to your house, so to speak, before it starts leaving its toothbrush in your bathroom.

For me, inner trust grew exponentially as I learned to partner with all aspects of the self. Partly because, in response to my invitation, the divine self promptly brought over a dozen suitcases and a houseplant—I clearly felt its steadily growing radiance taking up residence within. (And that felt nice.) But there was something else, too. I was also feeling more inner trust because I'd become trustworthy in the eyes of the subterranean self. I'd grown up. I had stopped avoiding inner discomfort. I'd proven I was here through thick and thin, no matter what.

Consequently I began to find it quite natural and obvious that divine wisdom should spring forth from within—where else? Nowadays I hear, see and feel inner divine wisdom. I also receive communications from the subterranean self with equal ease. It's no problem telling them apart.

For one thing, the subterranean self has no desire to play the role of trickster anymore. It trusts me to pay attention when it speaks its needs, even though it recognizes I may not give it what it's asking for. Nevertheless I believe it is certain of my underlying love and respect.

But even if it were to deviate from this partnership of ours, I would still unquestionably know the difference. And that's because I have come to understand so much more about frequency and vibration than I once did.

Divine Love is a frequency. Divine Light and pure, present-moment Awareness are frequencies. The same goes for divine wisdom, which always teams up with the Light of Awareness, and often with Love too, depending on the communication topic at hand.

These frequencies are felt in unmistakably recognizable ways as they interact with (and as) my own vibratory field. In short, I know in every atom of my body, mind and energy field what divine inner wisdom feels like. The Light of Awareness is alive within me, its divine wisdom now recognized as my own. It could never be faked.

I also know what communication with the subterranean self feels like. It feels more like the 'me' I wrestled with for so long: Sticky, judgey, vulnerable. These days, bless its beautiful heart, it also carries the sweet energetic signature of a trusting child that tucks its symbolic hand in mine as we go for a walk together. Even though we both realize this particular walk is headed off a cliff.

When we reach the cliff's edge it's highly possible the subterranean self will fight bitterly for its life. Or maybe it will simply surrender with a quiet sigh. Either way is okay. Either way this adventure of getting to know the self has, quite unexpectedly, been an honor.

Divine inner wisdom is everybody's birthright. Clairaudient talent is not required. What is required, as I see it, is the patient development of inner trust. As that process unfolds, you learn to trust quite naturally in the divine wisdom that's been waiting all along for permission to take up residence as you.

I suppose it might seem pretty weird, this idea of divine wisdom *as* you. Heaven walking the Earth as you. It sounds a little *Invasion of the Body Snatchers*-like, doesn't it? The personality self gets violently stripped away, and some alien form of perfection inhabits your physical body instead of you. But it really isn't like that.

'As you,' just means you begin to recognize divine wisdom, divine Love, divine Light is welling up in you, as part of your own natural expression. It doesn't feel separate or alien from the rest of you in any way. You absolutely recognize this transcendent, high frequency stuff is not being generated by your personality self. It feels unmistakably divine in origin. And yet it is definitely arising as a normal, comfortable part of *you*.

You're not a pipeline, in other words. Divinity isn't passing through you on its way from one heavenly place to somewhere else, even though that may be how it feels at first. Increasingly, as trust and willingness grow, you discover more and more that you are it. Until, finally, and with your full invitation and permission, it is all you are.

Mistaken identity

Here are some things I know about you. You are completely insignificant. You, along with everything you believe and know, are no more important than the ant crawling on your window sill.

At the same time, you are a magnificent constellation of stars, an unfathomable mystery of beauty and wonderment. So unique, such an irreplaceable part of the whole, you are an exquisitely perfect expression of Life itself, just as you are right now. I know all this about you, because I know it about me.

Not all the secrets I was keeping from myself were stories of pain and darkness. The biggest big-ass secret of them all turned out to be the one I kept about my own true identity, and yours.

I was sitting out in the garden one afternoon, listening to the busy chatter of birds, and thinking of nothing in particular. Suddenly I was invited to step back from the 'Carrie' self, to view all of life from a more balanced, less biased perspective. It was then I became breathtakingly aware for the second time, just how pointless my personal point of view really was.

This revelation didn't freak me out like it did back in that Israeli marketplace. Back then it had come as a crushing disappointment. This time (although I still teared up for a second or two), I quickly adapted to the new gift. How wonderful, to suddenly be so much less attached to my own limiting point of view! This was cause for joy, not sadness.

I had good reason to feel joyful about reducing attachment to the personal 'me.' It was a direct effect of the past-life do-over, a few weeks earlier. That experience had rearranged my foundation in some indefinable way, and the shift it set in motion seemed to be ongoing. It felt intelligent. Like a living thing, it continued to blossom ever more fully within my consciousness.

In each day's meditation, I kept being drawn back to the profound gift I'd received, of being able to spend my final moments witnessing the crowd as divine Source. Day after day I rested in that glorious feeling. The crowd's dazzling holiness had been such an immense, all-consuming joy. In the experience of it, I had cared about nothing else. How they behaved was completely irrelevant. The effect of their actions upon my body meant nothing.

And this is why, despite the initial moment of weepy sadness a few weeks later, I was thrilled to detangle myself a bit more from identification with my own personal point of view. The evaporation of my personal viewpoint had been the very thing that made possible the magnificent perceptual shift into Christ vision.

As I had gazed at that jeering throng, I held no ideas about them or me. They simply were; I simply was. My biases, fears, preferences, judgments, opinions, prejudices, backstories and assumptions all melted away, leaving radiantly holy truth in their place.

In the vision, the release of personal viewpoint was spontaneous. I didn't consciously choose it. But over the next days and weeks in my morning meditations I started purposefully playing around with releasing all my own perceptions about everybody and everything, in order to witness them as the softly holy divinity of the rose-gold Light that I am.

First, I would start with me. Resting as pure divine holiness, I would single out some 'unfinished' aspect of myself, removing all context from it until only the simple witnessing of its inherent perfection remained. And I rested in that. Next, I would randomly choose a problematic person from my vast back catalog, and do the same for them.

Finally I would bring in a highly controversial corporation or public figure, and release everything I thought I knew about them, everything about my perceived relationship to what they stood for, everything about the harm they may have been causing.

I witnessed them entirely without my own personal point of view. Entirely outside the interpretations of the world supplied to me by the subterranean self. And I would then bask in their divine perfection, exactly as they were right now. I did it until I could clearly feel their holy, rose-gold radiance was my own.

The Fricken Map is Upside Down

*   *   *   *

This is uncomfortable territory for the subterranean self, the supplier of the personal viewpoint. Christ vision means we agree to keep only one arrow in our quiver, so to speak. Love is the one-size-fits-all response, no matter who or what we encounter. Soft, holy, perfect divine Love—the response that automatically bathes us in this same Love, every time we offer it to another.

To the subterranean self, who desperately prefers we keep our options open, having only the single arrow of divine Love at our disposal would leave us as naked and exposed as that be-winged baby Cupid. And not in a cute way. The self wants to keep us safe from hurt and harm; in its worldview, divine Love is the opposite of safety. The subterranean self would counsel there is nothing more dangerous than to offer divine Love to the wrong being under inappropriate circumstances.

When it comes to Loving those who don't deserve it, the very idea of stepping away from the worldview of the subterranean self feels outrageous at first. The suggestion seems ludicrous. If we're not letting the subterranean self judge and assess our worldly experience anymore, how will we recognize danger when others act like transgressors? How will we identify the bad guys?

In the weeks and months after that initial do-over, I went on to experience several additional aspects of Christ Awareness. No doubt these accumulated knowings constitute only about one trillionth of the full embodied Christ experience. Yet mystically, this divine state of Awareness is holographic in nature; in some small and incomplete way, I have intermittently witnessed and joined as one with the all. (Paradoxes. Go figure.)

So I'll share with you here, and periodically throughout the rest of the book, what I know of this magnificent Christed operating system. My purpose in doing so, is to shed some illumination on commonly asked questions about the motivations or behaviors involved in Christ witness. Why, or how, a Christ does what a Christ does. Maybe these discussions will help it all seem a bit less weird, a little less intimidating.

To begin with, to see with Christ vision is not a lobotomy. We don't turn into a blundering fool, blissfully unaware of the motivations of others. We're just choosing to witness the truth of who others are, which is the same thing as the truth of who we are. Through this recognition, we tap into our infinite power Source.

Yes, in worldly terms this other might be a vile human being or circumstance. Yes, they might be causing active harm to others. Yet we're aware our interpretations and conclusions about who they are and what they're doing, are the very things that would block us knowing the truth about them or ourselves. And so we choose divine witness instead. For all our sakes.

Never mind the oneness thing. Even if we've all heard it said a million times that we're one in truth. I am you, you are me, we are they; we're not only connected, we're the same organism. Blah, blah, blah. If that's not yet our firsthand knowing, its true implication doesn't quite hit home: To offer divine Love to another (worthy or not), means we automatically know all parties concerned are worthy and Loved.

Here's a more me-centric way of saying the same thing. To offer divine Love, whether or not our subject seems worthy of it, feels amazing. Our entire being is bathed in soft magnificence. We feel safe and cherished. Amnesia disappears; we recognize our own holy identity at last. In that pure divine moment, as infinite Love caresses us, we know without a doubt that divine Love is the only arrow we'll ever want to shoot.

To go back to our old habits of judgment, grudges and perception of enemies would feel terrible mentally, physically and energetically. It's no contest. We really do need to ignore the advice of the subterranean self on this one. No matter what it might say to try and dissuade us, the truth is, one-size-fits-all Love really is heaven on Earth. In a good way. A non-sci-fi B-movie-body-snatching, kind of way.

The Fricken Map is Upside Down

This choice to respond only with divine Love does not leave us defenseless in the face of potential danger, by the way. Divine discernment steps in to take the place of personal judgment, and does a damn sight better job of knowing what's what, than we ever could.

Here's a hypothetical: Let's say you're feeling all Christ-y, and you take yourself out for a walk through the city. At night, for some reason. You happen upon a dark alleyway, and notice a shady character loitering at the other end. You see him clearly. You are fully aware of how he experiences his own limited reality.

You are deeply aware of the violence he perpetrates upon his own spirit, by acting as he sometimes acts toward others. You feel compassion for him. You feel absolutely no fear. You witness this man as a being of radiant divinity, the same as you. Because that's what he is. At the same time, divine discernment makes you aware this alley is probably best avoided at this time. And so you choose another route.

Except sometimes the same hypothetical might go another way. Discernment and divine wisdom might cause you to feel called to go down the alley, specifically to interact with this man. If this is the case, it's not an arbitrary or ill-considered decision. It is taking place because the Christ as you knows itself through its joyful service to all. And it would be clear to you as you approach this man, that this interaction can only be for the highest good—even though you don't know whether or not your body and possessions will remain 'safe' from an egoic point of view.

Nothing is ever truly safe in the fear-based worldview of the subterranean self, bless its heart. Lack of safety is part of the subterranean job description. Yet when it is our indescribable honor to unleash Christ-witness of another's divinity, true safety (which transcends everything of this world) is ours. Hence the fearlessness—which, to an outside observer, might be perceived as recklessness, or even cluelessness. It is neither.

In those final moments of my execution vision, I had no fear or regrets about anything that had happened or what was to come. My physical circumstance was not only irrelevant, it was no longer even on my radar screen. I knew perfectly well what was about to happen. But I had far better things to do with those last few precious moments, than perceive them through the personal viewpoint of limitation and suffering.

Love. Peace. Fearlessness and total safety. And above all, the indivisible, radiant holiness of our shared divinity. When that's our only reality, walking down a dark alley toward a divine being—if that's indeed what we're asked by our own Christ wisdom to do—is a piece of cake. Every step is a joy.

What can I say? When the unified Christ is the one in charge...your priorities will undoubtedly change a bit. And you won't have the slightest regret about that.

The very best kind of self-judgment

Thanks to the do-over, I no longer felt any reluctance to allow all beings their spotless divinity, no matter what their worldly actions may be. (At least in meditation.) I knew it wasn't up to me to assign them their divinity. That party was already going on, with me or without me. Yet despite all this newfound conscious willingness, I still felt a disconnect. Meditation was transcendent, but daily life still seemed full of the usual criminal suspects.

Now, seven weeks later, I turned inward to observe my own body-mind-energy field. I gazed with compassion at the totality of the 'me' I believed myself to be. Clearly there were still unknown parts of this self who didn't know how to trust or surrender their sufferings. Given the choice, why would they not have opted to stay in the magnificence of our own divine identity? If they only knew how, they would surely already have done so. Because seriously, it was the coolest thing ever.

I turned toward these shadowy aspects not yet ready to let go of darkness, and rested with them in quiet rose-gold compassion. As we sat together in radiant stillness, I recognized these hidden parts would find it painful or scary if I pushed them to accept the magnificent Light of divinity. I was flooded with tenderness for their predicament.

A sudden inspiration dawned. Maybe I could find a way to offer divine Love to those reluctant parts of the unconscious self, without forcing divine Light upon them. I didn't want to ask the unconscious self to change. I asked only for the willing parts of the self to embody luminous divine perception, so we could unconditionally embrace these more reluctant parts. Our only motivation would be to Love the reluctant shadow aspects wholly and without reservation.

I wanted the unconscious iceberg to be free to stay exactly as it was, so no awakening-induced trauma might befall it. Yet at the same time I wanted it to experience itself as deeply Loved, and profoundly safe. I wanted it to feel its own perfect innocence, its own infinite worthiness, without being asked to conform or change anything about itself.

I didn't even know if what I was asking was possible. It seemed unlikely. I wanted part of me to embody wholeness, on behalf of some other split-off part of me. That's crazy talk. Yet I was sincere in the inspiration behind the request. I wanted to go first, to cliff dive into God, specifically because it was the greatest gift I could offer to the beloved subterranean self.

For the last couple of years I had been steadfastly assuring the subterranean self I no longer wanted to abandon it. I no longer wished to go first, in the misguided attempt to run away from it. Instead I repeatedly promised we would jump together, into the great unknown. Yet here I was, ironically asking to go first once again—but for a completely different reason this time. Now it would be my heartfelt honor to go first, on its behalf.

A few minutes later, having set all such questionable requests aside, I was resting silently as the rose-gold resonance of the Christ that I am. Suddenly a verdict was handed down (or up) from somewhere in the depths of my subterranean regions: *We have suffered enough.*

I gasped. Really? Suffering would no longer be a requirement for any part of this self? *We have suffered enough*: Not exactly a blanket 'not guilty' verdict, I nevertheless understood this unexpected reprieve meant the slate could now be cleared. I could start anew. How marvelous! How generous, to be offered such a priceless gift of renewal.

The rest of that day was filled with gentle peace and relief. I could feel, in the deep down regions that still held glowing embers, the burning seemed to have stopped in the wake of this momentous judgment. But to my dismay the peace and relief faded gradually over the next several hours. Within a couple of days the faint glow of still-active embers could be felt once again.

Deflated, I wondered if I'd got my hopes up for nothing. Despite being told I had miraculously managed to fulfill my egoic 'suffering quota' (as if that was an actual thing), here I was, seemingly back in the same old spot. The machine-child had been laid to rest, no longer processing her red hot coals of fear.

The Fricken Map is Upside Down

And yet that familiar internal pressure, distant and muted, could still be felt. I sighed. Maybe it simply wasn't possible for me to know true freedom. Maybe I just wasn't built that way.

I asked an age-old question then: *Is there something missing in me?* Did I choose a gaming scenario for this lifetime in which I'm almost whole, but lacking some kind of key component needed for permanent peace?

I used to whisper that dreadful question in the dead of night, afraid to listen for the answer. Back then it seemed too unbearable to contemplate the awful possibility I was defective or deficient in some crucial way, and could therefore never know wholeness. I couldn't face the terrible possibility I was stuck this way for good.

This time, I tenderly gathered up all parts of the self and quietly asked the question outright. Clear eyed, I sat for the very first time, with the actual possibility of missing pieces, as I rested in the compassionate Light of rose-gold Christed solace. Maybe it really was so. Maybe I could never truly know lasting peace or wholeness in this lifetime—even though I'd been told we'd suffered enough. I let go of all hopeful expectation, and rested quietly in the not knowing. And then I went about my business.

*   *   *   *

Missing pieces. I didn't know it then, but that rose-gold session of true acceptance set in motion something epic. A series of events wondrous beyond imagining—but not quite yet. My non-linear evolution would roll on for quite a while before that happened, as divinity offered me necessary bits and pieces of its perfect curriculum in perfect timing.

In the short term, I felt a different kind of shift take place right away. Over the next few days a curious sort of restructuring seemed to quietly occur.

I awoke late one night in the middle of a rip-roaring storm. Thoughts of global warming crossed my mind, as they sometimes had in the past. Climate change (or more specifically, rising sea levels as they pertain to this island nation) was one of a small handful of recurring worries in which I invested on a semi-regular basis.

Only in the past couple of years had I consistently refused to take the bait, recognizing my need to worry was a standalone thing that could be pasted onto any topic at hand. That global warming is a legitimately worrisome issue was beside the point. If climate change were magically reversed overnight, I would just shift my worry onto the next thing in line, because worrying was one of the chosen ways I preferred to expend energy.

I knew perfectly well that worry was a useless function, but I didn't know how to stop. Over the past year or two, however, I would notice a worry cycle as it fired up. Instead of buying into the worry itself, I trained myself to turn toward the aspect of the self that liked to juice itself up by worrying. *I see you,* I would say patiently. *And I love you. And we're not going there.*

I would still receive the semi-regular invitation to worry about something, yet I found it pretty easy in most cases, to decline the invitation. But on this night, in the middle of this storm, as thoughts of global warming flitted into my mind, I found to my surprise I couldn't worry. It almost felt like the worry thoughts were bouncing off my brain before I had a chance to decide whether to accept or reject them.

Then I realized the thoughts were not bouncing off me; their sticky magnetic properties had vanished. I simply was not attracted to worry. Nothing in me was drawing it in, so it had nowhere to land. Suddenly the discipline of choosing not to worry wasn't needed. How strange. How wonderful.

A day or two later, on a sunny car ride with Steve I found myself engaged in yet another one of those discussions about the state of the world. And I noticed, to my relief and amazement, I felt no temptation to get hooked in. For the first time ever, I effortlessly listened and conversed without judging or making anybody the enemy.

The topics were as polarizing as ever, yet my own polarity seemed to have shifted. Nothing felt sticky or magnetic. The act of conversation itself now felt satisfying and pleasant. It was all so natural, so easy, I couldn't help wondering why I'd ever found it challenging in the first place.

The world (or is it?)

That loss of conversational triggers really caught my attention. As my own perception lightened up, I began to notice more and more often, seemingly unrelated aspects of my world automatically taking on matching radiance—without changing a damn thing about themselves. Their radiance was mine, and vice versa. When they say the world is a mirror, this is really what it means.

My whole world and the life I live within it, are exactly the same thing. The 'me' that I think of as *me*, is the knobbly little peak of my iceberg. Contained within the rest of that 'berg is not only my own subterranean self, it also holds my world as I perceive it. The same, of course, is true of you. Or anybody.

The world outside us is a blank Etch-A-Sketch. We're the ones who assign it meaning by doodling our own pictures all over it. And that's strictly an inside job. We have no choice but to automatically scribble our own unconscious inner state onto the world we see out there, because that's how egoic perception works.

So the trick, and the immense joy of the game, as I see it, is to learn how to love and embrace every bit of that unconscious inner stuff, no matter what it looks like. When the inner is revered, the outer gradually starts to appear worthy of reverence too.

Or we can go on doing it the way we usually do, which brings the opposite effect. If we believe deep down we are deserving of punishment—and pretty much all of us believe it, to some degree—then we can only believe the world outside is deserving of punishment too. But is that true? How would we know? We're unable to perceive the blank slate itself.

The graffiti doodles we've created about the need for punishment completely obscure the otherwise empty gray screen of the Etch-A-Sketch. It's never about what we see in the world outside. The outside world is just a convenient and convincing scapegoat for our deeply hidden inner turmoil. The truth is, we would

The Fricken Map is Upside Down

have no punishment pictures available to doodle onto the outer screen, if we didn't already believe our inner world deserves it.

I know. It doesn't sound right or logical or fair. It never will. These are impossible concepts to reconcile from inside the egoic thought system. The subterranean self will never voluntarily choose forgiveness of the world, because it can't. It is incapable of perceiving a world without victims and victimizers. Its own life support system is built on a rock solid foundation of enemy consciousness.

So when do we finally empty our quiver of all the other arrows, and make that singular choice for divine Love? When we've had enough of playing the game of self-damnation. That's when we put aside our condemnation of the genuinely ugly things we see in the world outside, and humbly ask to be shown the world's innocence and our own. Because like it or not, they're the same thing.

We might do it today, we might do it three lifetimes from now. We'll do it when we're ready, because it's the only way forward. It's the only way to win this round and move on to the next game level. I hope with all my heart that we, as a species, do it sooner rather than later. Because, my dearest friend, we've suffered enough.

Carrie Triffet

NINE

The river of Life

One day in meditation instead of going within (a journey into innerspace, the portal into one's own infinite universe), I was prompted to do something a little different. As I began my meditation, I was redirected into the physical body instead. I was still technically within, but this time I was within the physical density of blood and bone and all the things that make up the physical organism.

I sat in present moment Awareness while fully inhabiting my own body. To my astonishment I realized this was the first time I'd ever truly done it—willingly, at least. Although I had many times engaged in breathwork (which brings a similar effect of full body presence), back then I had innocently used the breath to overpower the defenses of the subterranean self. I had muscled my way into presence. It was very useful at the time, yet completely unlike what I was experiencing now.

This time, full body presence was simply allowed by all parts of the self. No coercion was employed or required. The natural sensation of bodily presence felt surprisingly different, to one whose spirit had never before completely descended into the body.

It felt good. It felt healthy. I sat this way for ages, silently transmitting the message to all the cells of my body: *All is well.*

It is safe to be here now, inside this body. I sensed the cells were listening. I could tell they were getting it.

A couple of days later, as I began to meditate again with the focus on being here now inside the body, I was redirected yet again. While resting comfortably inside my own body in the now moment, I was prompted to merge this feeling of present moment physicality with the underlying capital 'L' Life force that is always here.

I was invited to surrender this physical existence to all-of-existence. To Life itself. Just as an experiment, to see how it felt to melt my daily existence as I knew it, into the safety and relaxation of Life's sweet flow. To find out what it's actually like to drop all resistance to what is.

Gurus talk about dropping our resistance to what is. The idea makes good sense to the intellect, but just try accomplishing it. I never could. My body was on permanent high alert at the very idea of getting too close to Life, too close to the here-and-now of what actually is.

Being here now, where I physically already am, meant I was finally capable of considering a surrender to Life itself. Life is more or less the same thing as Love-Light-Awareness. Or maybe it's more accurate to say Life is the alchemical creation, the end product, of Love-Light-Awareness at work.

Yes, we're talking about the same lowercase 'l' life that's full of dreary Mondays and rainy day boredom. The life you know (and maybe aren't all that crazy about) is the ineffable divine essence that unites and animates all things manifest and un-manifest. At its core, I mean.

In its truest form, Life is not the shit and complications and obligations that make up our day. That's just the stuff we pile on top of Life to obscure it. Our existence itself is the miraculous thing we're talking about here. Life is, essentially, another workable synonym for 'God.' No wonder we have such trouble surrendering into it. We're really not wired that way. But as the wiring gets dismantled and upgraded, surrender to Life starts to look surprisingly good.

One of the most important prerequisites for the wiring upgrade, as I said earlier, is acceptance of this now moment inside the body. It's the agreement to consciously inhabit the space we're already in. Agreeing to be where we are, can't help but give rise to an immediate sense of greater safety.

Touch into this pervasive sense of safety, and you'll notice you're supported by a much larger, uninterrupted field of security and comfort. Cradled within this sense of pervasive security, you're invited to relax and let go of control if you want to. But only if you want to.

The present moment safety you're feeling inside your own individual body, feels not unlike the way a single tiny droplet might feel as it's surrounded and securely held by a larger body of flowing water. In this now moment, your droplet could so easily choose, if it wanted, to join the flow of the benign and beautiful river of safety called Life. This joining doesn't have to be permanent; you can dip in and out anytime, while you're making up your mind. Life's invitation is always open. All you have to do is say yes.

Is it safe to give ourselves to Safety itself? More than I can express. Life, I was surprised to discover, is entirely trustworthy. Partly because it is divinely kind and Loving, functioning always for our highest good. But also because Life is our own true identity. We are surrendering to ourselves, entrusting our own divine wisdom with the supreme honor of carrying the individual 'me'—the limited me, that each of us currently believes our self to be.

In my next morning's meditation, I was prompted to start off in a joining pool. (I'll give you the full lowdown on the joining pool later on in the addendum.) I hadn't used the joining pool meditation in the last few years. It felt like a reunion with a dear old friend. I was reminded how much I truly love and trust that sweetly conscious water. As ever, I dissolved myself into the water until I clearly felt I am the water. And then the exercise took a new and different direction.

I watched as the pool-that-I-am became the infinite Source of a powerfully flowing river: The river of Life. I could feel the river was made out of all the same water as that of its joining pool Source. All the same safety. All the same Love. All the same me.

I flowed and surged along, knowing myself as the river's joining pool Source; as the river itself; and also as the one being carried along by the current. The profound sense of belonging (for one who has never truly belonged anywhere) was indescribable.

*   *   *   *

When we fully surrender to Life's flow, we become sort of a working model of the universe in miniature. Each one of our cells fully expresses the grand embodiment of Life's flow. We come to know ourselves as Life itself, even as we're simultaneously being carried along by Life. Nothing is ever being done to us, in other words, when we allow the river of Life to carry us as it sees fit. We're not a helpless bit of flotsam being dragged along by the current.

To agree to 'go with the flow' (even temporarily) is the most beautifully relaxing, nourishing feeling. To be carried by Life is not stressful. Even though we don't know what's around the next bend. Even though not all of what comes may be to our personal liking. (Because our own divine self knows best. And not all medicine tastes delicious while it's going down—yet the end result is always better than we ever dreamed possible.) Despite not knowing what comes next, the flow feels good. It feels pure and clean. It feels meant to be.

There's something else, too. When you tune into this flowing river of Life, our shared oneness will automatically start to reveal itself to you, like a spectacularly anticlimactic *duh* of realization. Life includes all. You'll feel this simple truth in your bones, in your energy field. It's almost too simple and obvious to accept, but go ahead and accept it anyway. Oneness really is as unremarkable as this.

Life flows in, as, and through everything everywhere. Tune into this ever-present Life force in all things, and you'll notice it never gets created or uncreated. It simply is. Bodies and structures that temporarily house it will always come and go. Yet the Life force itself remains, unchanged. And the river is always flowing.

Pirate ships of the almost enlightened

August 28, 2018
The other day while washing the lunch dishes, I suddenly felt a gentle shift of mind and heart. Out of nowhere, I became a living expression of service to all. Maybe I should back up and capitalize that: A Living Expression of Service to All.

It was so glorious! Such profound joy. Sticky self-absorption disappeared. In its place, every thought and every breath in every moment became gladly dedicated to the wellbeing of all. It was an incredible honor, a humbling gift, to be able to take on this role.

I felt my energy field respond instantly to the change. It wasn't just that my frequency moved higher, although that happened too. I could sense my field's usual semi-incoherent patterns of energy suddenly came together intelligently, to form intricate, interlocking geometric patterns of exquisite beauty.

I'd somehow entered a sacred realm of coherent frequency, in which I gained immediate access to some small portion of the God broadcast. And oh man, it felt unbelievably good. I can only describe it as the most softly ecstatic knowing of who I am, and why I'm here.

This narrowband slice of coherent, awakened consciousness stayed about eighteen hours before it faded out. Every bit of the God broadcast, as far as I can tell, is wonderful beyond words. And this was no exception. At least, that's been my experience so far. Thumbs up to all of it.

Funny, how the mind can rev itself up like a runaway train, stoking its own boilers with nuggets of pure bullshit. I ricocheted from blissful coherence to this, all in the span of a single twenty-four hour period:

August 29, 2018

Never mind how painfully aware I am, that the seeking of 'future enlightenment' is a hopeless, neverending quest. Forget all my training to be present right now, with what is. Dammit, I'm having awake-ish experiences!

Less than one full day later, and this is the sort of non-stop propaganda I'm getting now, from belowdecks on the dear old subterranean me-boat: I should celebrate, I should get super-excited, I should meditate extra hard every morning from now on—because permanent embodiment must surely be coming really-really soon! How soon? Really-really-really soon.

Except I know it's not up to me when or how (or even if!) these beautiful states all come together into one stable, embodied awakening. It will undoubtedly happen at some perfect moment in just the right circumstance of just the right lifetime, and not one second earlier.

But all that grownup wisdom doesn't seem to dampen the egoic enthusiasm. 'We're practically awakened,' shouts the subterranean self, high-fiving itself gleefully. 'Soon we'll know permanent inner peace. But not yet, of course. We're not completely ready for that. We still have work to do. Oh, yes. LOTS more work on all our unfinished stuff. But we'll heal a little bit more today, and grow a little bit more tomorrow. And any day now—yes, maybe even next month! Or next year!—enlightenment is bound to happen.'

Oh, self. You're adorable. But really, get a grip.

That vague sense you're 'almost there.' Sound familiar? Almost whole, almost healed, almost awake. (Almost fulfilled, almost peaceful, almost living your purpose. Almost-almost-almost.)

The subterranean self, bless its heart, is tap dancing hard. It's doing its very best to keep us happy and give us what we say we want, while ensuring its own survival for one more day. But here's the truth: There is no such thing as 'almost

The Fricken Map is Upside Down

awakened.' (Or almost any of those other 'endlessly becoming' states one might crave.)

When I experienced that shift into field coherence (where Life itself formed interlocking geometries of intelligent divinity), I got a small hint of just how different the God broadcast really is. 'To see like the Creator sees' is infinitely more profound than just a change of viewpoint, or even a change of frequency. It's different in every way from seeing through the eyes of the subterranean self.

Of course there is a certain amount of crossover, as we progress on our dream-journey toward awakening. The usual truth-blocking vision does grow steadily more transparent, as the eyes of truth exert ever greater influence. But until the eyes of truth are the only ones in charge, our vision remains hopelessly incoherent. And without coherence, the divine, full-body knowing of *All is well*-ness can't be activated. Not permanently, anyway.

The Pirates of the Caribbean movie *At World's End* has an interesting scene in it, where Jack Sparrow discovers how to reach the alternate realm of Davy Jones' Locker. In some ways it's a great metaphor for the enlightenment search, as imagined through the anxious eyes of the subterranean self:

After fruitless scrutiny of his map, Jack, with the help of his invisible advisor, realizes he's been reading the map upside down. (There's a lot of that going around.) So Jack methodically works to capsize the ship, because he has suddenly realized up is down, and down is up. He realizes Davy Jones' Locker will be found in some other entirely unknown spatial configuration from the one we're familiar with.

The ragtag group of (subterranean self) crew members on deck voluntarily help him rock the boat from side to side. Next the (unconscious) beings deep belowdecks start to cut loose the heavy objects that will help Jack in his quest to overturn the ship.

Eventually, with the help of nearly all crew members on board, he succeeds. The ship turns upside down, and everyone is now underwater. After an excruciatingly long pause

Carrie Triffet

in which they all wonder if they're going to drown, *the horizon itself* slowly overturns. Ocean becomes sky, sky becomes ocean, and the ship is set upright upon calm new waters in the uncharted place where Davy Jones rules the waves.

*   *   *   *

Of this much I'm certain: Until my horizon has permanently flipped, I'm not almost enlightened. Nobody is. We might be thoroughly engaged in rocking the boat, but we're doing it from within the thought system that blocks us from knowing the true, coherent orientation of our own inner sky and ocean.

Along the way, our incoherent subterranean thought system does become less and less prevalent. Less and less relevant, as the glorious, illuminated wisdom of the divine self grows more at home within us.

But the subterranean self's counsel—its whispered opinions, definitions and beliefs about everything it perceives, is still being listened to. The subterranean self is helping us make sense of our world, bless it, because that's what we're still asking of it. That function will continue until we stop asking.

Future fulfillment is a classic subterranean theme. The mechanism is the same, whatever the future goal. *I'll be happy and confident when I lose thirty pounds.* Or, *when I make partner at the law firm.* Or, *when I meet my soul mate.* It's the same promise of inner wholeness, adapted to the wishes and preoccupations of each.

If, like me, you have sometimes found the idea of 'future fulfillment coming soon' a hard habit to break, I'll share with you my own method for addressing that kind of inner storyline. In my case it's been all about future enlightenment. But the same method can help with any of the other future-based fulfillment fantasies as well.

With great love and appreciation for the subterranean self, I would begin my meditation by gathering all parts

The Fricken Map is Upside Down

of my self into the present moment. Here we'd rest quietly together in the rose-gold Light of Awareness, where no stories exist.

Initially the subterranean self might kick up a small fuss at the removal of its future-based fantasy. So I would lovingly but firmly hold us in the compassionate Light of present moment Awareness until all resistance melts.

Then I would embrace the subterranean self, and celebrate all the ways we'd already changed together, to make daily life freer and more satisfying for us both. I would offer it my heartfelt thanks for its role in this. I'd thank it simply for being, not asking it to change a thing about itself.

And finally, I would bask in the truth of what is. I'd bask in *All is well*, taking delight in the divine perfection of this moment as it currently is right now. A moment which includes, in this particular instance, a slightly anxious subterranean self who endlessly scans the horizon for signs of flipping, in hopes it will happen soon, really-really-really soon—but please God not yet.

TEN

Soul reunion

September 28, 2018
It's not the sort of mini-break vacation I would usually go for.
Adele has been traveling around Scotland. She spoke of the
sacred Isle of Iona as one of her destinations, and the very
mention of the word 'Iona' made my knees tingle. My knees!
I knew I needed to go.

The reason I would never choose Iona for a four-day holiday
has nothing to do with the place itself, which is lovely. It's the
fricken pilgrimage to get there. The Scottish Hebrides Islands, for
God's sake. The trip took sixteen hours each way, and required
travel by car; then plane; then car again; ferry; car yet again;
and a final ferry.

A missed or late connection on any of those legs would have
scuppered the whole enterprise. Who needs the stress? And yet
that's what we did, and although it had its share of near-misses,
the trip was sheer perfection. It changed my life.

Let me back up and tell you first about something I encountered way back in 2013, not long after the Thich Naht Hanh awakening. It will give you some idea of the enormity of what occurred on Iona.

One night in 2013 I was meditating yet again on the whole concept of enemies and forgiveness. Yep, it's been a theme for a long time. Anyway I suddenly found myself catapulted into an interior space I'd never been before, a region I later named The Universe of Hate and Rage. Unbelievably caustic and painful to witness, it was indeed as big as a whole universe—in fact it was my whole universe. I was dumbfounded to realize all of its violence was pointedly directed at me. Me personally. I was the target of my own infinite hate and rage.

But why? I searched my mind for possible reasons. What could I have ever done to make a whole universe this mad at me? It seemed excessive, frankly. And then I thought, well maybe it's not just about me. Maybe this belongs to the whole collective. Maybe we all secretly feel this way about ourselves and each other. So I asked the higher self, 'Is this mine or is it everybody's?'

The answer, unsurprisingly, was: Yes. (That kind of question always gets answered in an indivisible oneness sort of way. Accurate, but not terribly illuminating. Not at the time, anyway.)

Unable to speak or eat, I spent the next couple of days sipping water and staring out the window. I had no context in which to place this shocking display of hate and rage. Back then it never even occurred to me to try and engage with any aspect of the subterranean self, to ask it for further clarification.

In the years between then and now I'd experienced lots of aha epiphanies, lots of healings, lots of awakened moments. And yet every release, opening or awakening brought only partial peace, along with a vague sense I hadn't quite got to the bottom of things yet. A faraway sort of dull ache, a muted, ever-present agony still seemed alive somewhere deep within.

Was I missing something? Or, was something missing in me? Some key component necessary for wholeness? I kept returning to that question. I'd recently faced it directly for the first time, resting with it in the rose-gold Light of infinite compassion. Yet no answers had been forthcoming.

This was the question in my heart as Steve and I made our way to Scotland to meet up with Adele. The Iona trip held non-stop miracles from the time we arrived. The following miracle, which occurred on the final morning of our visit, is the one that changed everything for me personally.

Adele and I were chatting over coffee about my progress in writing this book, which was roughly half finished at that time. The book was shaping up to be a fairly radical departure from my earlier teachings. I mentioned feeling a little nervous about speaking my truth to audiences who knew me from back in the days before I'd let go of my map. I wasn't sure how warmly or coolly they might receive this new information from me.

'You're blurry,' she interrupted me. 'When you started talking about your fear of speaking your truth, it's like your energy field started vacillating between two different dimensions. I can't even see you.' We stared at each other in silence for a moment.

'Something is asking to come through,' she added after another pause. 'Some unknown part of you needs to express itself to you vocally. But it is urgently insisting it needs your permission to be ugly.' She paused again, feeling into the information being given. 'It is adamant about this. You must allow the sound it makes to be ugly.' I nodded my agreement and waited, breathless.

Adele has never received shamanic training. Nevertheless what came through her next was unmistakably shamanic. Placing one hand lightly on my leg, she used her own vocal cords to give voice to what my throat was too blocked, or too traumatized to express.

The guttural sounds tumbled out for several minutes: Strangulated. Rough, harsh, angry. Anguished. Terrified.

'This part of the self is deeply afraid of the Light,' she said at last, taking a sip of water. 'It feels you're moving too fast toward Light embodiment.' I nodded and wiped the tears from my eyes.

'It does not want to be forced to change,' she continued. 'Others forced your throat to close, eons ago. It's important now that you don't force it to open.'

I cried some more, gratefully embracing this unknown part of the self. I was so glad it had agreed to show up, whoever or whatever it was. I promised I would not force it to do anything it didn't want to.

The next morning we said goodbye to Iona, and began re-tracing our steps toward home. Arriving several hours later at Glasgow airport, Steve, Adele and I popped into Starbucks to sit down with a hot drink and write a quick record of all that had happened during our time together. When we got to the shamanic episode where she'd said my throat had been 'forced to close, so it was important that it not be forced to open,' Adele gasped suddenly, eyes wide, as more detail flooded her consciousness. She turned to face me.

'Your throat was not forced to close. You were forced by conquerors to use your Light—and your throat—for very dark purposes.'

The background noises of espresso machine clatter and general airport busyness faded into silence. Chills ran up my spine as all the cells of my body testified to the truth of her words. I involuntarily clapped my hand over my mouth.

'Look what you're doing,' she said quietly.

I willed my hand down to join the other one in my lap. Adele went on to recount the basic outlines of the story she'd just received. It was too big, too horrifying to wrap my head around.

September 29, 2018

It seems I was the leader of a community of powerful spiritual adepts. We worked with some kind of vocal technology of divine Light. Invaders took my community hostage. In a naïve attempt to save the lives of my beloved community members, I let myself be blackmailed into using my gifts of Light for destructive purposes. And then, when I outlived my usefulness, my community and I were slaughtered anyway.

As soon as Adele said it, I'd felt this information ripple through my field. This was it. This was the missing piece. I could sense now that the soul's pain had been so great, part of its consciousness had somehow ripped in two and been flung away into space. Like an entirely other self had become stranded in a different dimension. And a secondary self (me) was built on top of the empty wound.

Carrie Triffet

Funny, I'd heard the term 'soul retrieval' before, but I never knew what it meant. I'm pretty sure I do now. I don't really know what long-term effect this reunion will have. But I can feel the split no longer exists. For the first time in millennia, I'm all here.

Now that this aspect of the soul was back in the same dimension as me, some surprising things became apparent. It was not afraid of the Light for any of the reasons I assumed I knew. It was terrified my embrace of the Light meant the ghastly nightmare would repeat yet again.

It was afraid we would be hijacked and forced to use our Light for evil purposes once more, through my naiveté or foolishness. That I would again choose collusion with dark forces, in the hopeless attempt to spare the lives of innocents. So the closer I moved to Light embodiment, the more pain and terror it felt.

Suddenly I realized how arrogant and silly I'd been. This part of the self had been living in hell, in her own private universe of hate and rage, for who knew how many thousands of years. With my book-learned spirituality, I'd unknowingly spent decades trying to reassure her that her experience wasn't real and didn't happen—because only Love-Light-Awareness is real. Which is true, yes, but entirely beside the point. I understood now for the first time how unwittingly unhelpful and disrespectful my attitude had been.

She, unlike me, was a spiritual master of some kind. She knew, through her own personal experience, far more about embodiment of divine Light, and about her own true identity in God than I ever had. She knew perfectly well what is and isn't real; she was acutely aware that Love-Light-Awareness is the only truth. And despite all that knowing—or maybe even because of it—this unspeakable horror came to pass, bringing suffering on an unimaginable scale. And she'd been frozen ever since, in her own self-perpetuated hell of guilt and torment.

She had agreed to show up and 'speak' her guttural throaty noises through Adele, on the proviso that I not try to rush her, or fix or heal her, or judge her or attempt to influence her in any way whatsoever. At the time, I'd agreed immediately to the deal. I would not try to change her at all. I would let her be exactly as she was.

Yet this split off piece was undeniably the missing self I'd been yearning to know all my life. I knew in my bones this was the essential missing part that had always prevented true peace. She was clearly the one who had phoned Kurt in my psychotropic nettle dream, informing him she was on her way home to meet me at last. And now here she was. I could scarcely believe my good fortune.

That agreement not to judge or fix or heal her should've been second nature by this point; I'd had plenty of practice with allowing other aspects of the subterranean self to be exactly as they were right now. Yet presented with the brilliant gift of this sudden reunion, all my prior training flew out the window.

I was wildly impatient, excited as a five-year-old, to meet this long lost wounded self and help her get back on her feet. I couldn't wait for us to become intimate besties. I wanted it more than I'd ever wanted anything. And try as I might, I just couldn't seem to let that fierce impatience go.

Oct 1, 2018
It's like I've dreamed my whole life of having a twin sister to play with. She's this invisible pretend-friend I've been talking to forever. And then one day out of the blue I find out it's actually true. A real live twin, an identical sister I never knew I had, has been discovered inside a burning building on some remote island somewhere.

Suddenly I'm like a tiny kid again, and I'm so excited to meet her! I put on my prettiest dress, the one with all the petticoats and sparkly bits. I gather up my dolls and bring them to the hospital to show her. I can't wait to tell her all about me. Oh, the fun we'll have getting to know each other! She'll come to my tea parties, and we'll play hide and seek, and she'll sleep over and we'll stay up talking all night.

I walk into the hospital room and gasp when I see her. She is encased head to toe in bandages. 'All her flesh has been burned off, the nurse explains in hushed whispers, 'and most of her bones are broken.' The twin's eyes, the only unbandaged part of her body, are turned away, staring dully out the window.

I tiptoe up to the bed wearing my brightest smile, and introduce myself in a respectful whisper, as I know she's really sick and I mustn't shout. I try to tuck my favorite teddy bear next to her arm, to keep her company. He tumbles off the bed. I pick him up. I stand by the bed a while, uncertainly clutching the teddy and watching for signs she'll turn and acknowledge me but she doesn't.

I decide to try a different form of communication. I go away and draw her a great big pink heart with both our names in it. Then I draw another picture of the two of us holding hands under a smiley-faced sun. I lay the drawing pad carefully across her bandaged legs, positioned so she can see it. The weight of the paper pad causes her pain, and she moans. Defeated, I take the drawing pad away and go sit in the hallway to have a cry.

Finally I get it—but even now it's still a struggle. I really do have to let go of the agenda of this childish self who is so thrilled to meet her long lost other half. This one wants things the other one just can't give. Not yet, and maybe not ever. I so desperately want to play with her, together in the Light of our shared divinity. But that's the very last thing she wants or needs.

For her, at this point at least, Light hurts. I have to be genuinely okay with the fact that she is finally here with me, and that's enough. She may never come any closer. She may never choose to re-integrate. And that has to be okay.

But I ache. I don't know what to pray for. I don't even know what to hope for. Everything I want involves Light.

It took a number of days. In each meditation I labored over and over again to place all excitement, all impatience, and all desire to help or fix, onto the rose-gold Christ altar within. Eventually I got the hang of it, and thereafter spent each day's meditation resting quietly without hope or stories, as I bathed in soothing rose-gold solace.

I simply let the long lost twin be. Maybe in doing so, I was finally giving her room to breathe, I don't know. But almost immediately I could feel a fundamental difference. A different kind of wholeness.

Almost without noticing, I began to sleep through the night, waking up refreshed some mornings. I could count on the fingers of one hand how many times that had happened over the past twenty years, and never more than one or two nights in a row. Now, although still not every night, refreshing sleep was becoming part of the new normal.

October 5, 2019
The long lost twin still isn't saying anything, so I'm just going by how things feel. And they feel pretty good. Not, like, transcendently good. But pretty good, pretty peaceful. Pretty whole, relatively speaking. And that's a miracle in itself.

Two days later another wondrous shift occurred, this one also undoubtedly due to the soul reunion in progress.

October 7, 2018
Last night I awoke in the middle of the night with an unfamiliar feeling in my chest. My whole heart was operational. No shadowy sections still offline. And it was softly radiating divine Love. Wide awake now, I noticed my entire energy field radiated the same Love. Curious to find out where this field of Love ended, I moved my Awareness to the world outside the bedroom window and discovered it, too, radiated Love. In fact there seemed no boundary where this personal field of divine Love trailed off and the world's Love began. I was part of an unbroken energetic field of Love. I knew myself as this endless field of Love for maybe four hours before the knowing faded gently away.

All the spiritual teachings point to this truth of indivisible divine Love. I just never personally experienced it before, because it kind of requires a fully functional heart. Or at least a heart with all portions present and accounted for.

I guess this brief experience was yet another of those narrow-band slices of the God broadcast, a heads-up that my heart was now resonant to the frequency of divine Love. This is what I'd been praying for, all those years. And now, since the return of the 'missing piece' the previous week, the persistent heartache of fragmentation seemed to be gone for good.

This was a different kind of integrated oneness than I had ever imagined, one having little to do with spiritual awakening. All parts of me (even one in very rough shape) were reunited at last. Or at least cohabiting in the same dimension. That reunion alone brought a lifetime of suffering to an end. And now, the ultimate gift on top of it all: My heart could feel. *Really* feel.

* * * *

My dear friend Leni enjoys an unusually simpatico relationship with subterranean selves. They allow her to speak for them, making possible a kind of communication that can help bring greater cooperation and understanding between the surface self, and the submerged iceberg. Years ago, frustrated, I once asked her to ask my subterranean self what was up with my ongoing inability to fully access higher feeling states of the heart.

Ever since I'd started a serious spiritual path, feelings like joy and bliss had always felt curiously muted. And of course throughout most of my life, divine Love had been a complete non-starter. I demanded to know why. She tuned in, and reported that my subterranean self was showing her an image of itself with one foot firmly on the lid of a large metal strongbox. *Yep*, it assured her confidently, *I've got those feelings right here.*

At the time I didn't know what to make of that answer. The subterranean self had actually seemed proud of its ability to hide those feelings away from my consciousness, despite my desperate ongoing attempts to access them. The more I thought about that foot on the strongbox lid, the more resentful I became.

Only now did I begin to understand. Unlike me, the subterranean self had always been aware of the existence of that fragmented missing piece of the long-lost self. So it responded

The Fricken Map is Upside Down

by blockading, or insulating itself as thoroughly as it could, to minimize the agony I might feel from this intolerable condition. And yes, it locked those associated feelings away in a strongbox guarded night and day, lest I inadvertently open a portal of unimaginable horror before I was ready for the potential consequences.

No matter how much I may have wanted the firsthand knowing of joy, bliss and unconditional divine Love, there would have been no way I was ready back then to experience my own reunited, fully operational heart. It would've required a level of self-forgiveness and forgiveness of enemy transgressors, far beyond what I was capable of at the time.

October 19, 2018
How perfect life is. How divinely these events are timed, and with such elegant precision. Without knowing it, I'd been craving wholeness all my life. This nameless drive to somehow put myself back together again was the reason I embarked on a spiritual path in the first place. Yet had this soul reunion come to pass even a few months earlier than it did, my trust, faith and love for all parts of the unseen self (higher and lower) would not yet have been strong enough to handle it.

In fact the unfolding reunion would continue for several months beyond this initial point. Along the way other brilliant miracles of forgiveness would first be required of me. In perfect right timing, divinity unerringly wove its rose-gold path of Light and Love throughout my consciousness. Patiently, gently, it offered the perfect lessons, again and again, each one a vitally needed stepping stone toward wholeness and freedom. At the time this progression felt quite random. Looking back, it was anything but.

True Service

October 27, 2018

A few days ago in meditation, I was prompted to invite in the higher self of a friend who's been suffering with acute pain. I was prompted to also bring in the higher selves of those who were struggling to care for her, so I did that too. I brought all four of them into the rose-gold Christ resonance, to rest together with me in perfect compassion.

A statement rose up spontaneously from the silence within, addressed to these four people: 'Give all your suffering to me.'

A pretty startling statement, but I decided I was okay with it. In response to this invitation, each person revealed the nature of their own personal suffering, and to whatever degree they were prepared to release it, the Christ as me received the offering gladly.

The last person in line indicated the nature of his suffering was that he didn't feel safe in his body. I let him know I would be honored to receive his physical unease. At this point I could dimly feel my own subterranean self in the background waving its little arms in alarm, like, 'No! We've had a lifetime of feeling unsafe in the body, and only recently have we got rid of that feeling! Don't take on more!'

In response I gathered up my sweet subterranean self and brought it in, to rest in the same rose-gold resonance with the others. To this self, it seemed inconceivable we were volunteering to burden ourselves with other peoples' unwanted crap—let alone specific kinds of crap that might damage us. But that really wasn't what was happening at all.

'The rose-gold Christ self has unlimited capacity,' I explained patiently, 'and nothing gets taken on. Nothing is a burden. To receive the gift of another's suffering does not mean I keep it. The suffering is welcomed into me and then it just sort of fizzles out, in the Light of divine truth.' The subterranean self fell silent and let me hold it in rose-gold solace. And there we all stayed until the end of the meditation.

The Fricken Map is Upside Down

For the next few days my morning meditations were mostly spent receiving the sufferings of others. Who those others were, was sometimes sparked by an awful news story, or sometimes it was inspired by the circumstance of people I knew personally. Or sometimes it was just a general prompt to hold the entire planet in the Light of rose-gold compassion.

I will describe more about this action of receiving the suffering of others, to give you an idea of what it's like, and how it happens. And why I would agree to do it. Because it kinda sounds crazy otherwise. Like something nobody would ever want (or be able) to do. Right?

It's true, a personal self could never do this. It is entirely the province of the divine self. The first several times this kind of meditation happened, I was always prompted to begin by sending the me-self to go sit in the corner, with a coloring book or something. And in that temporary space where I wasn't witnessing through the personal lens, the Christ self, the divine self, had room to ooze through and blend seamlessly into my consciousness. For the duration of the meditation, the divine self became my primary conscious Awareness, to whatever degree I was able to sit back and let it arise. This is what allowed me to see more like the Creator sees.

Letting Christ vision arise feels natural and good, by the way. Letting it arise feels safe. Part of seeing through the divine lens means everything is automatically recognized as holy— which means nothing and nobody is on the attack, including me. Safety is.

Furthermore, everything is recognized as being indivisibly part of capital 'L' Life itself. Even the things we don't think of as technically being alive. From the divine perspective, Love-Light-Awareness is not theoretical. It's the obvious divine identity of everything in existence and non-existence.

All is God, in other words, and it's an incredible honor to serve God in whatever form is currently being suggested by the divinity within. This recognition of the divinity in all, highlights the deeper meaning of soul reunion—it's just a way bigger soul than most of us realize. And good Lord, does that reunion ever feel good.

So when yet another tragic mass shooting has occurred, for instance, this is what it looks like to the divine self in charge of my meditation: All concerned are held as one indivisible holiness. None are seen as more or less holy than the others.

I witness the shooter who spouted virulent hate slogans even as his bullet-torn body was being dragged away by police, and I am prompted to receive his suffering. It is an indescribable honor to do so. I receive it equally alongside the suffering of the ones who died in terror, and the communities that grieve.

When I'm in that space of rose-gold Christed compassion, I witness that shooter in my meditation and I only see a divine being acting out in terrible pain and confusion. I'm aware of his actions but there is no judgment. I see him as the divinity he is, period. I feel only compassion for that which ails him. So I invite him to puke up his darkness, his hate, his rage and fear. It comes to me as a universe of caustic fury, every bit as immense as the one I experienced back in 2013. I receive all of it gratefully, yet none of it touches me.

And here's the thing. Christ wisdom knows receiving the pain of others actually has some kind of huge long-term healing effect. I don't know why that is; the being, or planet, in question may never experience this healing relief consciously or directly. Nevertheless, the Christ as me knows beyond all doubt. Profound permanent healing occurs. So profound, the mind can't grasp it.

By the way, what I said here about the action taken to deal with the shooter applies only if I've heard about the shooting after the fact. If the Christ-as-me hypothetically happened to be present as the tragedy was unfolding, a different sort of divinity-infused action might perhaps arise. So let's pause here for a minute and talk about what it means to 'turn the other cheek.'

In my universe, 'turning the other cheek' has to do with Loving and welcoming the societal ill or transgressor. Love and welcome means our response holds no vibratory signature of resistance or misdirected attack. We are deeply honored to be witnessing God, even though God is currently expressing as obvious harm. If some of that harm is aimed toward us, it doesn't make us back away in self defense. We need no defense, and we know it. Our energetic field radiates this knowing.

Turning the other cheek does not preclude us from taking appropriate action to stop a transgressor, if that's what is required. So if we are present while that aforementioned shooter is methodically picking off pedestrians, and we ourselves happen to have a gun and know how to use it, now would not be the time to engage in lofty spiritual speechifying about the sanctity of all Life. That shooter obviously must be stopped, for his own good as well as everybody else's. So we aim our gun, with greatest Love and compassion.

He is God expressing as confusion, rage and outward-directed pain. We welcome all that he is, exactly as he is, while doing everything in our power to make sure his killing spree is shorter and less damaging than he intended. Our action to stop him is motivated by our profound mercy, not only for his targets but every bit as much for the grievous predicament of the shooter himself.

As I see it, 'turning the other cheek' is an oblique description of how the synapses fire differently, once our perception has been drained of the personal, me-centric lens of enemy consciousness. To turn the other cheek means we offer our infinite mercy again and again to the one who, driven mad by his own pain, is on the attack.

We witness him in his true divine perfection. It's a holy action that in itself shatters paradigms and rearranges worlds— even as we simultaneously twist his arm up behind his back until he drops the weapon.

In our eyes the shooter is the Beloved, both before and after his gun is taken away. Turning the other cheek, when properly understood, is not an expression of codependent doormat-hood. Nor is it a state of passive denial. Turning the other cheek, my friend, is badass.

November 29, 2018

As ever, this stuff mainly happens during meditation. It's not like I go through my day automatically broadcasting rose-gold emanation. I try not to be impatient, or skip ahead of myself, but sometimes I can't help it.

Who knows, maybe 'Walking Christ' will be my job description at some point. It'd sure look swell on my LinkedIn profile. But right now I'm still me. More confident, a little wiser and a lot more compassionate toward self and others. Noticeably less frightened of what people think of me. But other than that, basically I'm the same 'me' I've always been.

Yet at the same time something expansive and wonderful is starting to flourish within. Every day more Light is finding a permanently embodied home in here, and it feels so good, so incredibly good. There are no words to describe it.

I want to take a moment to point out how naturally this process has unfolded, because (unlike in previous eras) this gradual transition between operating systems is anything but frightening. Or at least that's been my experience.

Unlike the all-or-nothing Christed embodiment of pure white-gold divinity, this rose-gold resonance of the unified Christ seems to allow for gradual training wheels and Lovingly supervised practice sessions, as I learn to ride my wobbly God-bike.

As my confidence grows in my own ability to 'balance the bike,' my deep-down cellular fear of the unknown is lessened. And as the fear drains away, space is created where yet more of my own luminous divine identity can be recognized firsthand. Which in turn creates more confidence and more balance. It's a very gentle process.

December 3, 2018

Plenty of aspects of daily life still feel unfinished or unhealed, although my focus has somehow shifted away from the me-centric universe I once inhabited. My unfinished stuff no longer occu-

pies the throne of ultimate importance, which is kind of a relief. It's here but it's just not that big a deal anymore.

As I offer Christed solace to all who need it, the still-functioning subterranean self snuggles next to me in rose-gold safety and watches it all in silence. It seems resigned to this gradual changeover of operating systems, and it has more or less stopped resisting the process.

This, I believe, is what comes of loving and respecting the egoic self with all our heart and soul. Historically this changeover of operating systems has always been described as a brutal struggle between equally matched adversaries. Yet that's clearly not how it has to be. Kindness breeds kindness. Respect brings respect. Love your own subterranean self like your life depends on it, and it will surely return the favor, to the very best of its ability.

January 9, 2019
There are so many different shades and styles of awakening. For some people, the initial awakening remains forever static. Having 'arrived,' there's no place else they'd want to be. For others, awakening is an ever-deepening, ever-expanding journey into pure embodied divinity.

Some awakenings are all about realizing true mind; others are unquestionably heart-based. Some drop into the void, others never go near it. The whole thing is a big mystery. A dreamer's dream within a dream, about awakening out of dreams.

I honestly don't know where Christ knowledge fits into the great flow chart of awakened consciousness. Is it higher than some kinds of awakening? Is it lower than? Is it off in its own cosmic cubbyhole somewhere? Dunno. Don't really care. I just know, for me, the Christ Awareness symphony is what's currently playing on my radio, and the tune is glorious. I can't help but hum along.

And I surprise myself by admitting my very favorite part of the symphony so far, is the 'service to others' thing. That's something

I never saw coming; I've never been a fan of others. Who knew total dedication to others would end up being the ecstatic icing on the holy cake?

*   *   *   *

Let's talk some more about this business of service to others. Divine service is an intrinsic part of the Christ operating system, so it's worth trying to understand it as deeply as possible. It might be helpful to start by looking at what it is, and isn't.

In its truest form, divine service to others is never found in physical doing—but it certainly doesn't preclude it. (Again, Gandhi is a useful model of this. No passive accepter of the status quo, he.)

True service and physical service can, and sometimes do, take place simultaneously. But they're not connected. Physical service on behalf of others is a greatly needed activity in this world, obviously. It would be ridiculous to suggest otherwise. It just has nothing to do per se, with the coherent transmission of embodied frequencies of pure divine Love-Light-Awareness.

The selfless actions or behaviors we tend to associate with awakened saints sometimes come about as a natural knock-on effect of having recognized the divine in all things. So a person might awaken and, as a result, choose a life of working with the poor, as one example.

But as I've said, the divine realization itself and this type of worldly expression aren't technically related. Service in the physical realm is never mandatory, because true divine service can only occur through being. It's automatic and constant. There is no doing involved; doing is an optional extra.

If you're a (regular, un-sainted) person who feels naturally drawn to physical service, that's wonderful. I'd still recommend true divine service for your aspirational bucket list. Just imagine the added power, when your physical doings are infused with the infinite true service of divine being. The exponential good you'll be able to do in the world will truly know no bounds.

The Fricken Map is Upside Down

But I mainly want to address here those of us (like me) who do not feel called to join the Peace Corps, or devote our lives to physical service. I'm talking to those of us who are afraid if we allow divinity a foothold within, God will surely ask us to sell the condo (and we love the condo!) and traipse off to do volunteer work in malarial jungles on the other side of the world. Where there are snakes and things.

So much confusion and trepidation exists around the imaginary requirements of selfless Christed service. Maybe if we demystify it a little, this will help reduce some of the fear and general misperception surrounding the idea of service to all. So let's get more specific about the difference between doing and being—and then look at how that might play out in a hypothetical daily life scenario.

To awaken to Christed perception automatically shifts our focus into divine service. The needs and wants of our own individual (subterranean-inspired) self are now seen as will-o-the-wisp ideas without substance or meaning. To give them no further attention, is not a sacrifice. We're too busy being deeply in Love with the totality of our own divine self, which includes all others. Service to all has become our joy, our honor and our privilege. It's more fulfilling than we ever could've dreamed. It's all we want.

Christed perception automatically includes service to all. These are indivisible aspects of the same divine frequency. But devotion to service does not mean volunteering in soup kitchens or mosquito-infested jungles, unless we are inspired to do that. (And if we're inspired, it means we truly want to.)

It doesn't mean giving away all our money, time or gifts to everyone who asks, unless that's our genuine inspiration. Again, if it's our genuine inspiration, that means the giving of these things will feel wonderful. But if we're not inspired, it's not what we're meant to do.

Herein lies much of the anxiety about Christ embodiment, and all the imagined downsides that come with it. In truth there are no downsides. An embodied Christ is not a self-sacrificing doormat.

Think about this for a minute. To know yourself as the Christ is divinity breathing itself alive as every moment of your evanescent physical existence. The infinity of God is running through you, operating as you. Which is pretty much the opposite of a doormat, wouldn't you say?

Stripped down to its essence, the embodiment of Christ perception is the recognition of divinity in all things, period. This embodied knowing causes our field to radiate the magnificent coherent frequency of divine truth. We don't work to radiate this potent energetic frequency, it's our natural expression. It is our being. It is also the most profound—perhaps the only—true service we can ever 'do' for another.

The energetic frequency of the divine operating as you, connects with the energetic field of everything you encounter. Your field, which is emanating its own true divinity, connects with the field of another and reminds it of its own true potential as well.

The other's field may or may not choose to take your reminder and run with it at this time. Whether they do or don't is irrelevant. The power of your divine frequency isn't dependent upon anybody else's response to it. It's almost as if a sort of heavenly electrical circuit is completed, every time the divine operating as you witnesses the divine identity in another.

This action of the divine recognizing the divine is catalytic in ways far beyond anything you or I could ever know. Stuff changes at mental, emotional, energetic and even physical levels as a result—but not in predictable or linear ways.

The work your field engages in, here, where you live, may profoundly change somebody's life on the other side of the world. Or it may seem to have no effect right now, but could show up as a mass movement for liberation fifty years from now. The Christ as you, knows the catalytic power of its own divine emanation. It needs no visual proof to know this is so.

So yes, the Christ as you might very well be drawn to engage in volunteer work that promotes the physical uplifting of your fellow humans in some kind of visible, ongoing way. Interacting with them has, after all, become a source of deeply solemn joy for you. But maybe that's not what you're drawn

The Fricken Map is Upside Down

to do. Maybe you're a musician, and you feel called to sit in a studio day after day, bringing the divine resonance of your joy into your musical compositions for all to hear.

Or maybe you're a school janitor. And your service is the profound Love you radiate as you empty trash bins and mop the floors every night. In some ways this is also a blend of doing and being. The physical structure of the school itself is altered, its vibrational frequency rearranged through its nightly interaction with your divine energetic field. You're not doing it intentionally. It's just what happens while you're going through the motions of performing your work. This can't help but impact students and faculty alike, in ways you may never know. Service comes in an infinite number of guises. It doesn't have to look like anything you currently recognize.

To expand on the theme of non-sacrifice, let's explore a hypothetical scenario of doing and being, as it might occur in daily life. Let's say you, one who has awakened to embodied Christed perception, are rushing to catch a plane. As you dash through the airport, someone recognizes you from the teaching videos you've posted on YouTube.

This person stops you and begins to pour out their sorrows in the expectation of receiving your patient and deeply caring advice. They have felt the radiance and resonance of your Love firsthand on video, so they naturally assume their suffering is your number one priority to the exclusion of all else. And in some ways they're absolutely right about that; you know this person is God, and God is indeed your top priority. Therefore this holy encounter, like all encounters, is met with your limitless compassion. Yet if it is your requirement to be on that plane, nothing says you need to miss your flight in order to acquiesce to this demand.

You, simply through being, are already performing true service for this person. Your energy field has been doing its thing all along, gracing this one and every other nearby with its benediction. As you listen to the person speak, your field automatically witnesses this other in their divine perfection, embraced in Love as the God-self you are.

It's not a decision you've made to be nice, or act spiritual. There is no choosing your response. To a Christed one, Love is the only response and it's automatic. It's who you are.

Joyful service is also who you are. If inspiration suggests lingering with this one is more helpful than gracing that particular airplane flight with your energetic presence, you don't question it. You miss your flight to be of service here. There's no stress or anxiety about re-jigging the schedule. You flow with, as, divine will in every moment.

But if lingering here is not your inspiration, you don't question that either. You respectfully explain you have a plane to catch. And without waiting for the other person's permission, you move on. In this particular case, if indeed making that flight is the requirement, resuming your hasty trek through the airport is the only appropriate form of doing.

The interaction itself, thanks to the effect of your energy field upon the other, is life changing and paradigm shifting. That you have not also satisfied their innocent egoic expectation of how a selfless Christed being is 'supposed' to behave, is of no true consequence one way or the other.

A budding friendship

February 28, 2019

It's common gardening knowledge that trees should be pruned during dormant winter months. If buds are already forming on healthy, happy branches, conventional wisdom says, you've waited too long. But this winter was a mild one. Trees formed buds in early autumn, then stayed wide awake and juicy all winter.

Hazels, willows and alders all grow like mad here, most of them adding six or eight feet to their height and circumference every year. Our acre would soon resemble a densely shaded woodland if we let the trees go unpruned. Beautiful, but not so great for raising tomatoes.

We consulted a friend who enjoys a warm relationship with Nature spirits and the natural world in general. She advised us to give the trees twenty-four hours notice when we intended to prune. Besides being the polite thing to do, she said, this would give the trees time to withdraw their sap from the branches to be cut.

I tried it with a long row of willows. The day after silently informing them of my intention to prune, I began working my way down the line, secateurs in hand, lopping off branches. The cut branches seemed fine; healthy but not weeping. I didn't think too much about it.

On the fifth tree, I cut a few branches much like the others. Inexplicably, the next branch I cut oozed volumes of sap. I gasped in dismay. One single branch forgot to withdraw its sap? Wasn't it paying attention when I gave notice the day before?

I apologized to that branch and the tree it came from, then gingerly resumed my pruning chores without further incident. No other branches showed signs of sap loss.

I later realized the single oozing branch had been shown to me as a teaching demonstration. I hadn't fully believed in my ability to be heard by trees when I'd warned them of my pruning intent. And when I began to cut their branches, I noticed their sapless condition, yet still didn't really believe it had anything to do with my warning. I had nothing to compare it to. Maybe these trees just weren't the sappy type.

I wouldn't have realized my twenty-four hour notice had produced any effect—until I was shown what a normal spring-time branch looked like when cut. That must have meant a single branch from willow number five had volunteered to take a bullet, so to speak, allowing its lifeblood to dribble out so I might learn the lesson.

I was humbled, grateful for the generosity. There's so much I don't know. After that I tried to give proper notice, each time I meant to prune or trim or dig something up. But English weather is variable at best. I'd give the trees clear warning I intended to come back to prune them in twenty-four hours, then it would pee rain for five days in a row. So that line of trees would be left dangling, presumably wondering whether to move their sap or not.

Other days we would suddenly be graced with sunny weather. *Screw it*, I'd think, *I'm going in*. And I'd grab my secateurs, apologizing as I worked. All through the winter and early spring, I apologized a lot.

One day I was methodically cutting back a row of massive evergreens. They sat directly in front of a second line of spindly deciduous trees, blocking all sun and hogging all nutrients. Undoubtedly the evergreens had been planted years ago as small bushes, meant to provide eventual year round privacy during those months when the trees behind them weren't in leaf. Fifteen years later, I thought it might be a good idea to try and rescue the beleaguered trees in the back row.

Behind a radically trimmed evergreen, a sad looking, moss-covered tree gradually came into view. Many of its bare branches looked dead. Without thinking much about it, I set about lopping off its dead bits. I trimmed low-growing branches to improve airflow around its trunk, while I was at it.

'You're brave,' Steve said quietly, watching me as I worked.

'Oh?' I glanced quizzically over my shoulder. 'Why's that?'

He gestured toward the tree I was pruning. 'That's an elder.'

I froze. I am new, as I've said, to Nature spirits and the lore surrounding them. But even I was aware of the mighty reputation of the elder. (Google it if you're interested.) Last summer I steered clear of all our elders, except to admire their beautiful flowers and berries from a respectful distance. No way would I have lopped off this one's branches had I realized, let alone without giving notice or asking permission.

I later spoke to my Nature spirit/tree pruning advisor, and confessed what I'd done.

'You should pack up and leave the country immediately,' she replied, only half joking. But then she followed it up with some wonderful advice. 'If I were you I'd go out on the land and have a sincere conversation with Nature itself. Explain what you've explained to me: That you're a slow learner, that you made a mistake, and that you'd love to be taught more. Ask for Nature's friendship.'

The following day I sat down inside one of the greenhouses on the land, and spoke to Nature from my heart. I admitted my shortcomings, apologized for my many mistakes and thanked it for the extraordinary patience and kindness it had shown me thus far. I asked to know it better. I asked if we could become friends. I didn't receive an answer, but I wasn't expecting to.

The day after that I was digging up invasive weeds and brambles from a large stone planter bed, in preparation for transplanting some early-flowering perennials we'd purchased for overwintering bumblebees to enjoy. As I worked carefully to tear out long ropes of bindweed without damaging the herbs and bushes growing nearby, I pondered this crazy human insistence on assigning relative value to some plants more than others. Or some bugs more than others.

Lavender good, bindweed bad. Ladybugs good, aphids bad. Bees super-duper good, hornets not so much. It made me think of the helpful and harmful fungal networks, some of them promoting beautiful vitality, others destroying their hosts. Was one type actually better than the other?

I wondered then how Nature itself perceives all the living beings in its care. Would Nature feel any preferences based on a species' usefulness or prettiness? Would it be dismayed by one species' destructive tendencies, or delighted by another's symbiotic behavior? Would Nature ever assign relative value to one species over another for any reason—or are we the only ones who do that? I wasn't asking anybody, just idly musing as I worked. My thoughts often ran this way as I toiled in the garden.

I was astonished when a soft feminine voice answered my question. *All of Life is the Beloved*, it said.

This majestic statement was accompanied by a deliciously gentle wave of unconditional Love for all beings; this experiential wave of divine Belovedness filled my mind, body and energy field. Dazzled, I set down my tools and paused to luxuriate in the unexpected gift, before resuming my chores.

I worked in silence for a minute or two, cleaning up straggling rows and preparing carefully chosen areas for the new transplants. *And how does Nature see humanity's obsessive quest for order and control*, I asked? *Our insistence on growing flower gardens in tidy beds as we like them, not as the flowers themselves would ever choose to grow naturally?*

The answer this time carried a twinkle of gentle amusement: *Humans are the Beloved, too*, it said.

As is often the case with divine communication, a whole world of unspoken contextual information was transmitted on the energetic carrier wave behind those two simple statements of Love. This type of communication is felt firsthand throughout one's own energy body; when I was shown Nature's attitude about something, I felt its perspective as my own. Here is the larger unspoken explanation, as I received it.

Nature makes no distinction between species. It would never judge one more desirable or important than another. Life is one grand, indivisible thing. (At this point, I felt the immensity of Life's grandeur as it swept through my field). Life's true divine identity is known, celebrated and cherished. Nature is in Love with Life. Nature *is* Life.

The individual species within Life's great unity are all completely free to behave as they will. That's part of the deal. Their expressions and behaviors are allowed equally; to Nature, the quality of these expressions is irrelevant. The magnificent divine identity of all Life is what matters.

Although my questions about order and control were relatively innocent, garden-related ones, they were asked with an unspoken subterranean subtext. I was asking from within a perceptual framework that took for granted large-scale human transgression upon other species, upon each other, and upon the Earth itself. This unspoken subtext was addressed as follows:

Each species, even a very transgressive one, is free to be as it chooses. (I felt this total freedom throughout my field.) Because my questions had included helpful and harmful fungal networks, I was next shown the example of Dutch elm disease, a fungal pathogen of great power and efficiency. I was able to experience its consciousness directly.

I recognized the intention of the fungus is simply to thrive and multiply. It is unconcerned about what this means for its beleaguered hosts. I saw and felt that Nature peacefully allows this and every other form of behavior.

I next felt the purity and power of Nature's Love for the fungus itself. As this experiential wave swept through my field, I radiated with the firsthand recognition of fungal divinity: The fungus is God.

Nature does not play favorites among individual living beings, or groups of beings. None are mourned in their physical passing, none are celebrated or protected to the exclusion of others. To our eyes, these natural forces at work may often look like tragedy. To Nature, the same event is seen as perfection in action.

The wave of unconditional Love as I experienced it here was completely dispassionate about this process of destruction and renewal. It was accepting of all, allowing all to be as it is. To Nature, the bodies and structures that temporarily house capital 'L' Life are of no consequence. Only Life itself is valued, and it is valued and cherished more highly than we can comprehend.

And PS, the contextual carrier wave informed me, humans are not in a separate category of the damned! Despite its blanket assurance that *all* Life is cherished equally, my innate sense of separation had still led me to automatically assume 'all Life' means everybody except people. As if we, as a species, are somehow not part of Life, or part of Nature.

As this second answer and its accompanying wave of Love and inclusiveness caressed my field, I was suddenly made aware of the hidden guilt I carried on behalf of humanity. I held us apart from Nature because we, as a collective, did not deserve to be included. Because we are despicable. Irredeemable. I hadn't realized I felt that way, until Love quietly unearthed the belief and held it up for me to see.

As I basked in the energetic vibration of all-pervasive divine Love, I played around with forgiving myself and all of humanity for what we are. And I felt something crack open. Not a lot, just a little.

Later in meditation, I sat quietly with this newly unearthed core-level unforgiveness of humanity. Breathing rose-gold Love and Light, I held the human collective softly in silent Awareness.

An image arose in my mind. Humanity was symbolically shown to me as the garden soil, and my own roots within that soil appeared as charred, blackened stubs. Present, but not really part of the ecosystem. I was given to understand I had cauterized my own roots to protect myself from humanity's dreadfulness, but in doing so had cut off all nutrients and support.

I saw then we've all done some version of this to ourselves (some of us more emphatically than others). All of us isolate our own roots to some degree. It's part of how we maintain a sense of separation from one another and from the divine.

I held my blackened roots in silent Awareness and softly breathed rose-gold Love and Light. I noticed the black ashes were illusory; as soon as I saw this, the ashes fell away effortlessly, simply due to my rose-gold conscious attention upon them. Underneath the previously charred casings, delicate white roots appeared.

Tender and vulnerable! Whispered the subterranean self in dismay. *Don't we need to be strong?* To the subterranean self,

The Fricken Map is Upside Down

the toxic soil of humanity seems full of enemies: Predatory bugs and hungry animals, soil-borne pathogens and invasive weeds—any one of which could overpower our defenseless roots. They could steal our nutrients, or they might kill, eat or damage us in other terrible, unknown ways.

The higher self responded, *Tender and vulnerable, yes. But let indwelling divinity handle the strength part.* Within the energetic transmission of this divine answer, I could feel just how radically different its proposed operating system truly is.

I contemplated going without protective egoic armor of any kind, in my interactions with humanity. Could I dare to be truly defenseless? With *people?* I acutely felt my own defenselessness. My own nakedness. I was willing to entrust my tender roots to the dangerous 'soil' of humanity if only I could crack the unknown question mark of how, exactly, to receive divine invulnerability as suggested by the higher self. I hesitated, trying to work it out intellectually before having to commit.

Indwelling divinity can't operate on a permanently embodied basis unless you forgive the soil and let your roots merge with it, I was reminded gently. Oh. Right. Of course. I had to be willing to let the soil be innocent, without lining up all my defenses just in case it really wasn't.

This proposition wasn't something I could intellectualize beforehand. It made no logical sense to merge my undefended roots with humanity as a whole. This could only be agreed to as a leap of divine trust.

Out of nowhere an unexpected wave of grief crashed over me. In it, I noticed for the first time the great loneliness—the overwhelming homesick feeling of separation from my Source, separation from humanity, separation from Life itself.

So I took a breath and said yes. Even though the subterranean self still warned it was a bad move. I took that naked leap of faith—even though it might mean death or worse for my skinny little roots. And in that 'yes' moment, hitherto unknown chambers of a much wider heart expanded and came to Life.

Carrie Triffet

Rose-gold breath

For months I'd been working with various aspects of the rose-gold frequencies, and had been enjoying their effects upon my meditation practices. During one such meditation session, the inspiration bubbled up to infuse the breath itself with rose-gold. It felt wonderful. My morning practice then became to simply sit with the rose-gold breath, noticing it, allowing it to move throughout my being. Within a few days, inspiration once again popped in, to begin breathing conscious rose-gold breath through a troublesome issue I'd brought into the meditation with me. And that's when things really got interesting.

Everything began to accelerate when I added this simple practice of conscious rose-gold breathing, not just during my meditations but also throughout the day. Maybe this fast-tracking occurred partly because this practice brought me out of 'hypothetical' meditation mode, and into the real-time choices and expressions of daily life.

When I noticed I was becoming triggered by a person or circumstance, the rose-gold breath quickly became my go-to evolutionary tool. I found this real-time exercise to be a quick and effective method for stepping beyond enemy consciousness, in the moment when it counts. I'll give you an example.

Some months ago, Steve and I were working out on the land, when we noticed a farmer two fields away, his tractor spraying billowing clouds of Roundup onto his field. 'Chemical plowing,' they call it. Never mind the widely publicized scientific documentation of catastrophic species loss here in the UK over the past few decades, or the predicted eco-collapse of this island nation.

As I watched the tractor, I recognized a trigger arising: I don't like Monsanto or its products. I didn't react to the trigger. Instead I brought only the neutral word 'Monsanto' into my mind, and I held it there as I simply breathed rose-gold through it for several seconds. I dimly felt the divine helpfulness of this choice.

After several seconds I no longer felt the Monsanto/Round-up trigger, but I noticed I still felt triggered by the farmer who uses it. Again, I didn't react. (*Humans are the Beloved too*, I reminded myself.) Instead I brought the neutral idea of local farmer consciousness into my mind, held it there, and I breathed rose-gold through that.

I sensed this was an immensely powerful exercise, yet it's hard to describe, even to myself, why that is. Did my actions bring substantive change to anything about Monsanto? Or farmer consciousness? That's beyond my current knowing.

But I no longer require seeing any sort of visible change before my eyes, to know God is the only power, and only truth is true. It was enough that I recognized divine helpfulness of some kind occurred, through my choice to breathe non-reactive rose-gold. So I guess by working with rose-gold breath in this way, I brought some substantive change to *me*.

This harks back to our earlier discussion about appropriate action taken singly or in groups, using the example of beach cleanup. Rose-gold breath works beautifully in this regard. Prior to the cleanup activity, we might each set an intention that our rose-gold breath be an ongoing prayer for healthy beaches and healed oceans. Then as we fanned out on the beach we would reverently pick up whatever has washed ashore, all the while focusing only on the rise and fall of our own rose-gold breath as it moves through the objects being picked up. It's a supercharged practice that's catalytic beyond measure, I suspect, and directly instrumental toward the active creation of a beautiful new world.

Carrie Triffet

Integration

April 12, 2019

Late last night after settling into bed I saw an image, an invitation of sorts. I was shown the remainder of my 'unconscious' iceberg—only this time it held one lucid, wide open, fully conscious eye. Neither friendly nor unfriendly, it was gazing steadily at me. It seemed to be saying, 'You wanted to see me? Here I am.' I knew this was the long lost twin, making contact at last. I said yes to the invitation. 'God, yes. Hell, yes. Please show me everything.'

The image shifted to a murky seabed. Rivulets of dark viscous liquid—blood, I supposed—streamed through the water in billowing underwater curls. I watched them peacefully as they dispersed, gradually staining the seawater red. The imagery paused; did I want to see more? 'Yes, definitely. Whatever it is, I'm ready for it.'

In response my mouth filled with an unmistakable flavor of thick, metallic liquid. 'Oh I see,' I thought calmly. 'It's my own blood.' The imagery paused again. Did I want to go on? 'Absolutely. I welcome all secrets, whatever they are.'

My vision was then turned heavenward. The sky was an eerie orange color, cloaked in thick, turbulent clouds of brownish smoke. With this visual image I received a delicate unfolding of the rest of the twin's story: I was witnessing the end of civilization as I knew it. And I was partly responsible.

I was allowed to feel her overwhelming grief and remorse, but only as the faintest wisps of present-day emotion. Just enough that I would fully comprehend her plight, without adding fresh trauma for her or me.

I saw the work she had agreed to do for the conquerors had been taken away and somehow weaponized. No other details were offered. I was left to wonder: Did she know her work would be used to help destroy her own civilization? From the comfort of my modern day armchair, I would like to think she'd have refused to collaborate had she known, bravely choosing certain death for herself and her community of adepts, rather than be party to full scale genocide.

The Fricken Map is Upside Down

Yet who among us can say for sure what we ourselves would do, if faced with that situation. As I experienced the faint wisps of her overwhelming self-recrimination, I realized it didn't matter whether she was technically complicit or not. She was utterly convinced of her own guilt, then, now and forever.

I realized I alone held the power to end her torment, on her behalf. In the rose-gold Light of divine Awareness, I welcomed and embraced full responsibility for the tragedy. I accepted all guilt, the knowing that I myself am the bad guy. I steadfastly met her exactly where she believed herself (and therefore me) to be. No more resistance. No more refusing the inner enemy.

 Logic makes no difference in these deeply embedded pockets of cellular memory. There would have been no point in insisting to her that she didn't mean to do it. Or that she was only doing what she thought was best under intolerable circumstances. Instead I opened up and welcomed all self-accusation, all hate and rage. As I did so, I felt layer upon layer of ancient, locked-down energy lift up, release and dissolve from my body and field. Layers whose existence had been unknown to me, before they vanished.

Something curious happened in the wake of accepting that I am the bad guy. Within a day or two I began to feel a strange sort of kinship with bad guys everywhere. Don't get me wrong. I have no more desire to be an evildoer now than before. But because I no longer resist the terrible 'truth' about my own irredeemable guilt (and have therefore been redeemed of it), I no longer perceive evil ones as 'other.'

I don't like what they do or what they stand for, any more than I did before. Yet now they are no longer held apart from me, in stubborn denial of our shared Source. Allowing evildoers into oneness is no longer a theoretical exercise; I've truly set the Etch-A-Sketch aside, on this one. On some energetic level, I genuinely feel and know I am they, and they are me. Funnily enough, it's a huge relief.

This emancipation from energetic lockdown was the start, not the end of the integration process. With these formidable layers of energetic defense no longer in place, the mental-emotional-physical self was ready and able at last, to address and release its deepest, most painful unconscious beliefs.

The process began as the separated shards of my enemy perception quietly started knitting themselves together into something resembling wholeness. It brought in its wake more effortless clarity than ever before. I started to notice once again the gratingly unpleasant core of my egoic thought system, but in a completely different way this time.

I was not affected by its unpleasantness. I was not sunk within the experience of it. This time I witnessed it from a higher perspective, with an attitude of deepest compassion. I noticed I was feeling no desire or need for fluffy blankets to hide its ugliness from my consciousness.

In this newfound well-knitted clarity, I noticed for the first time the conscious personal 'I,' (the 'me' I think of as *me*), really *is* the ego. There is no 'me' and 'it.' I had already known the conscious 'me' operated through the same lens and was part of the overall egoic structure. But those fluffy blanket layers had seemed to keep each segment of the egoic self cocooned quite separately.

Only the splintered perceptual lens itself makes any of us believe the inconvenient subterranean region of the self is somehow a separate inner 'other,' an unwanted roommate we seem unable to evict from the premises. I noticed I am unmistakably one singular, gratingly unpleasant bundle of miraculous divinity. From the top of the conscious self to the bottom of the iceberg, I am all of it, seamless and united. Let's call it the 'me-go.'

It was a relief to notice this. I also noticed the me-go is inert and without independent power of its own, unless I continuously choose to blow the breath of life into it. With deepest gratitude then, for this shadowy nothing self that I am, I slipped into meditation and surrendered all of me into the rose-gold Light of Awareness. And there I rested.

A few days later I began to sense more aspects of the twin's trauma surfacing for release. These aspects didn't seem able to do it on their own; although the energetic prison gates had opened and dissolved, the prisoners themselves still seemed to cower in their 'cells.'

I realized deeply embedded unconscious ideas were still being held within the cells of the physical structure. Yet now as never before, I sensed the way was unobstructed by barriers of any kind. Total release from ancient suffering was now a possibility.

As I was preparing to sit down for an exploratory meditation, a faint spike of the old food addiction fizzled like a damp firecracker through my consciousness. *Shouldn't we eat something to cover up the pain?* It asked wearily, knowing its argument would be rejected. In a rush of tender clarity, I suddenly saw the addiction from its own point of view. And I realized I owed it an apology.

I had always assumed the addictive-compulsive voice was insane. It wasn't. *Food is our safety, it's our only friend*, was an accurate statement from its perspective. Food was its only reliable tool and ally, for keeping secrets from entering my consciousness. The only illogic was in the insistence the addictive behavior would bring relief from pain. And even that, I now realized, wasn't entirely illogical.

The subterranean self knew full well the agony warehoused in the cellular body and the three lower chakras of the energetic body. By keeping that region groggy and preoccupied with digestion, it knowingly traded one form of despair for another, somewhat less devastating kind. It did the best it could to make the intolerable tolerable. And it did it with the best tools it could cobble together at the time.

Over the next few days I simply rested with the rose-gold Light of Awareness inside the cells of the body. Now that the protective energetic barrier layers had been lifted, I discovered these formerly unreachable parts of the self awakened readily to themselves. 'Readily' doesn't mean 'easily.' It means I found out at last what their problem was.

I saw the terrible conundrum, the central splinter embedded in mind and heart. It was reflected in the consciousness of each and every cell:

Love and Light are dangerous weapons.
But Love and Light are good.
Is good evil?
Is God evil?
How can I ever know whether God is trustworthy?
And me—I'm made of God, too. How can I know if I'm trustworthy?

The answers can never be found intellectually. Is Love innocent? Is God innocent? Am I? For me, resolution came another way, for other reasons. I had already experienced several small slices of the God broadcast. Each of these temporary experiences of Christed consciousness had acted directly upon my energy field and cellular body, lessening their terror. Each of them had testified to the knowing that God is good. That helped a little, but frankly not a lot, in this critical decision-making moment.

I was motivated more by the pain and exhaustion of indecision. It's very hard work, as it turns out, to endlessly tapdance on the tip of a dagger. I realized I'd been refusing to commit one way or the other, seemingly for eons. I just couldn't do it anymore.

I gave in, even though these core questions of God's guilt (and therefore my own) were still operating within my cellular consciousness. I surrendered anyway. War over. Even if it would mean, potentially, that the bad guy won.

Instantly upon surrender, the nervous system relaxed. Muscles stopped their constant tensing. And heaven and hell breathed a singular, well-knitted sigh of relief at last.

Postscript

A river runs through it

May 3, 2019
It's hard to describe the changes that have come in the wake of that surrender. It feels kind of like the indwelling Christ wisdom and I have taken our relationship to the next level. No more living out of suitcases; inner divinity has brought over its living room furniture.

I can only marvel at the change. After a lifetime of being commitment-phobic with God, I suddenly seem to have no problem whatsoever, with letting divinity move into my old cramped, poorly lit apartment.

Now that I've given it a set of keys to the place, so to speak, I'm thinking I should probably just let rose-gold divinity build me a whole new house instead. I mean really. What's so precious about the old place, anyway? It's small and shabby. I never even liked it.

What a relief it is, to no longer feel unconscious dread of the divine, or secret mistrust on a cellular level. I like God; God likes me. What's the big deal? Far from being resistant, I'm overjoyed, at the idea of letting my home and world be rebuilt by a divine architect. I look forward to a magnificent dwelling. Or rather, a magnificent indwelling.

*   *   *   *

This business of learning to embrace Life makes for an interesting journey, don't you think? It's an incremental process of deepening trust, and inevitably, the pace is uneven. It takes as long as it takes, to embrace divinity and capital 'L' Life, instead of the (comparatively cramped and poorly lit) life we've known. Sometimes the pace of progress can seem a little bit discouraging. Sometimes the progress seems like anything but progress.

In the beginning, internal subterranean resistance is fierce, to the very idea of sharing inner space with a divine roommate. It's all about hanging onto the illusion of personal control, personal privacy, personal autonomy and especially personal safety. (None of these are real, but we very much like to pretend they are.)

We also hang onto the even weirder idea that whatever we have now, no matter how comparatively paltry it may be, is worth protecting from the magnificent Love that wants only to embrace us with infinite goodness.

So at first we're stingy with our trust. We don't want divinity getting too close. We want to see other people—literally. Separation, and all that comes with it, is what we prefer. It's what we feel we need to survive.

The gradual increase in trust is what brings clearer vision. Through clearer eyes we recognize we're not actually losing anything valuable by welcoming our own indwelling divinity. The opposite, in fact. Clearer vision, in turn, brings deeper trust. Like I said, the process is uneven, and it takes as long as it takes.

When our vision clears enough, it suddenly becomes obvious there's nothing about the old house and its contents—the old controlling self and its precious baggage—that's worth protecting. It's all junk. It's always been junk. We realize we've only been clinging onto it all so obstinately because, in the absence of abundant inner Love, safety and fulfillment, our meager treasures felt like consolation prizes we couldn't afford to lose.

Clearer vision shows us there's nothing at all to fear in a house that's designed and built from endless Love. Clearer vision makes us idly wonder what our problem was. Why did we ever bother resisting goodness? What did we imagine we were being forced to give up in exchange?

Learning to embrace infinite Love, safety and peace is no sacrifice. Releasing the subterranean-generated personal viewpoint is no sacrifice. Resting in Life's flow is anything but a sacrifice. It's just like the gurus have always said.

If you're ready and willing to believe all this now, that's wonderful. I rejoice with you. If you're not quite ready or willing yet, that's wonderful too. Your timing, as always, is miraculously,

The Fricken Map is Upside Down

non-accidentally perfect. When you're ready, you'll know. When enough trust and clarity have accumulated, the decision to stop restricting divine access to your inner apartment is quickly followed by the joy of turning over all Living accommodations to the divine architect within.

There's more to true spiritual freedom, of course, than simply surrendering subterranean control to the divine house builder. There is the matter of allowing divinity to be as you. So let's talk a little more about the process of coming to recognize yourself as Life, being carried along by Life itself. Yep, back to the river we go.

In learning to trust in Life's divine flow, you could say it's an incremental process of setting aside the navigation maps, the life vest and finally the oars. But again, none of this is a sacrifice.

The map is set aside as we look around at our life and it dawns on us that, although we followed directions diligently, we're really not where we imagined we'd be by now—and we haven't the faintest idea how to get there from here. (Because it turns out we've been holding the fricken thing upside down. Or...maybe sideways? Or back to front. Not sure.) Once we've figured out we're no good at reading maps, we discard them gratefully and ask for a different navigation system.

The life vest is symbolic of our endless attempts to protect ourselves against an unpredictable and unsafe world. Whether we guard our hearts against relational wounding, our health against illness, or our homes and businesses against fire, theft or 'acts of God,' (Ha! Good one) the craving for safety is woven deeply into the consciousness of the human collective.

Yet shit still happens, despite our safeguards. When we get good and tired of being perpetually fearful, we give the life vest back to God. It never really worked anyway. It was just one extra thing to wear. And after it's been taken off, we're startled to notice how much Lighter we feel. The removal of the vest is more of a relief, than a sacrifice.

The decision to set aside the oars, with its implied surrender of power and control, requires the most trust of all. To not be in charge of deciding when or how we flow, is a frightening idea to the one who still values independent movement. But eventually we notice insisting on self-determination is very hard work. By definition, it means traveling against Life's current, always out of rhythm with our natural Source.

At some point we relinquish the oars gladly, and discover how great it feels to rest for a change. Everything about this river's flow now feels so safe and welcoming—and we can't help but notice Life's flow is far better at navigation than we ever were.

And that's when we realize we have the option of releasing the rowboat itself. It's hardly a sacrifice. We no longer see any point in fighting to remain separate from the river of Life. *I like God; God likes me. What's the big deal about holding myself separate from Life itself? Why did I ever think that was a good idea?*

We stop resisting Life's divine flow, and little by little we start to know ourselves as the river of Life itself. Herein lies the ultimate safety. No matter what sort of challenge may lie around the next bend, we know we are secure—because it's impossible to drown, when you know yourself as the water.

To know yourself as the river of Life is to know spiritual freedom. To know yourself as Life carried along effortlessly by Life itself, is to claim your own sovereign birthright of being. It is the end of subterranean suffering. It is the clarity and confidence that comes from trusting deeply in who and what you really are. And you, my friend, deserve nothing less. We all deserve nothing less.

So I hope you'll consider letting divinity build you a new house. It'll be way nicer than any dwelling you ever dreamed of. And I likewise hope you'll let Life itself carry you in its river currents, until you come to recognize you're inseparable from the water.

Growing ever more comfortable with the river's deep, trusting flow is a process that's only indirectly connected to enlightenment, by the way. I'm not sure permanent awakening is even relevant here. It doesn't seem to be a requirement. Learn to Love and trust all parts of the self through whatever means feel resonant for you. That's the requirement. That's the pre-requisite for learning how to surrender to Life's majestic flow.

So that's my heartfelt desire for you, for me, and for everyone. May your brilliant new house be built by infinite Love, and may your housewarming party be awesome.

May you be inspired to let the river of Life carry you where it will. And may all parts of you, from the very low to the very high, learn to genuinely enjoy getting wet. Until finally, *wet* is all you are.

ADDENDUM

Doing and being

For those of us who have always looked to other teachers and teachings to shape our own experience of God, liberation means, in part, that we no longer feel a need to search outside ourselves for spiritual guidance.

We already have, and are, all we need—and when we start to feel into this truth and receive direct knowing of the divinity within, we can more confidently begin to trust the authentic inner wisdom that's always present. As trust grows, inner strength and spiritual freedom start to blossom at the same rate. It's a process that is incredibly empowering. The primary job as I see it, therefore, is to activate that inner trust and knowing, so the true self can start to make itself known in our daily existence.

As the divine self is slowly given more room to make its radiant present felt within, our daily 'doings' become more and more infused with the wisdom of divine being. To facilitate this evolutionary process, the following section contains meditations, exercises, related teachings and commentary. It also goes into more detail about my own journey and the effects of these practices upon it.

The meditations and exercises listed here act as a sort of chronicle of my own progression over the last couple of years. I offer them as a breadcrumb trail for anyone who may be interested.

Most of the practices are listed in approximate chronological order, more or less as I received them. Of these, Awareness and presence (the first of the major exercises) are the two most important meditation skills to master, as they lay the foundation for all that comes after.

FINDING EVIDENCE OF DIVINITY WITHIN

Only as I look back now, do I realize the primary lesson behind every exercise inspiration I received, was to teach me to recognize the divine self already existing within me. The higher self had, in fact, been patiently leading me in this direction for many years. As much as I would've preferred, at times, to assign all evidence of luminous divinity to outside forces, I was always ultimately redirected to find the eternally radiant Source within.

This inner radiance wasn't always obvious, to put it mildly. Sometimes I had to investigate quite deeply in order to find any hint of the divine within. But I now see how vitally important it is, to recognize the divine self that is always already here. Not just as an interesting concept on paper, but (to whatever degree possible) as a palpable part of daily reality.

Over time, this proactive approach toward inner divinity has brought with it a subtle yet profound reordering of my worldview. I've found a deeper relationship with my universe, and a different knowing of my place within it.

A welcome side effect of this change is that the divine is now much more easily perceived within the chaotic experience of daily life as well. I still have my moments where I'd rather not participate in the world's madness, but I no longer turn away in dismissal. My inner foundation now seems to include a clear recognition of the magnificent divinity, hiding in plain sight, within each person in every moment. This makes it so much easier to refocus my attention on the miraculous truth of what is, and to remember compassion for the crazy me-gos we all are.

This section aims, therefore, to help cultivate not only a strengthened knowing of one's own inner divinity, but also an enhanced sense of the miraculous nature of existence itself.

Toward that end, let's look a little more closely at Love, Light and conscious Awareness, the three raw materials of divinity. They are the fundamental building blocks of this grand universal mystery and as such, they are employed throughout the exercise section. Yet Love, Light and Awareness can also be recognized as wispy echoes within our own mundane experience, if we know where to look.

1. Awareness

Look back on any moment of your life. Are you aware of it as you're thinking about it now? Were you aware of it at the time? The answer to both questions has to be 'yes.' Awareness, the first of the fundamental building blocks, is a normal, everyday part of our own true nature. It's nothing we have to seek after, because it's here all the time.

There aren't two different kinds of Awareness, the Special Spiritual Kind and the normal kind. It's all Capital 'A' Awareness. It's all divine, and it's always present and functioning. It just might take a little practice to notice its divine attributes, if you've never paid attention before.

Try this: Pick a nice moment from your past and revisit it right now. It doesn't have to be big or dramatic, just let a pleasant memory spring to mind.

Relive the sights, the sounds or smells, the emotions, the weather, who said what to whom. Take your time and recall all the details. Immerse yourself as deeply as you can, in everything you remember about the scene...

While you were fully occupied with reliving that scene from the past, were you also noticing your surroundings in the spot where you're sitting? Were you focused on the ticking of the clock, or listening for sounds outside your window? Probably not. You transported your Awareness to a different time and place. And because it wasn't here or now, the details of your current reality faded.

You've actually been time traveling. You've been on an out-of-body adventure. Human beings do it all the time. We think it's perfectly normal, and it is. Yet because it's so easy and normal we dismiss its miraculous nature. We call it 'imagination.' We call it 'day dreaming.' Like it's nothing special.

I bring this up to point out a couple of important things. One: Your Awareness is not limited to being where your physical body is. Awareness is free to go anywhere, and does. Two: You are a magnificent, multi-dimensional being. Your universe of time and space is your playground. When you project your thoughts into the past or future, or even sideways into some other place in the world, you routinely shift your Awareness from one timeline to another, one dimensional possibility to another. All from the comfort of your living room sofa.

Awareness has always been a ready tool in our toolkit. And that's why it's no big deal. There is nothing to attain we don't already have in plentiful supply. It's more like developing a muscle. It takes a little bit of practice to intentionally locate Awareness in the present moment, because we usually use it unknowingly to navigate other imaginal realms.

When Awareness is explored with conscious intention to know it better, its divine aspects automatically start to blossom. The higher self seems able to use our intentional explorations of Awareness as a sort of highway system within the mind, sending divine wisdom and inspiration more easily into regions that may have never accessed it before.

Intentional Awareness is somehow mystically imbued with radiantly holy Light, which is the second raw material of divinity. This Light of Awareness heals by its simple presence. Working with the Light of Awareness is the foundation, or jumping off point, for many of the exercise explorations in this book. It's also a worthy practice all by itself. Whenever something troubles us, we can simply rest with it in the Light of Awareness.

Nothing is required of us beyond this humble witnessing. In fact, if we were to try to label, add to, or 'fix' whatever is being witnessed by the divine Light of Awareness, its infinite sweetness would evaporate with our meddling efforts. It's never us doing the work. We're just connecting with this particularly accessible aspect of our own divinity, energizing it with our focused presence and then getting out of the way. The Light of Awareness does the rest.

2. Love

Awareness is a readily accessible aspect of our own true nature, now that we know where to find it. But what about Love and Light? Possibly not quite as obvious. We'll take a look at Love first.

Capital 'L' Love bears no resemblance or structural connection to what passes for love in this world. For one thing, real Love is not an emotion or feeling state. It isn't given or withdrawn based on circumstance. Real Love is a permanent identity that embraces all it witnesses, excluding nothing. Its presence is unmistakably divine in origin.

Although our worldly version of love is not made of the same stuff as divine Love, paradoxically we can temporarily experience a little bit of Love's glorious divinity if we happen to find ourselves deliriously swept up in worldly love. An ecstatic heart throwing caution to the wind, is like an uplifted bounce on a heavenly trampoline. It can help us temporarily approach the very high frequencies where divine Love is known.

Our worldly in-love-ness, therefore, takes on a magical shimmer around the edges, a gloriously soft radiance I now recognize as a telltale calling card of divine Love. Nothing else about the in-love-ness is divine in nature, of course. The whole romantic episode is a tango danced between two subterranean selves. How could it be other? Not to be a buzzkill, or anything, but I'd be lying if I implied worldly love could ever truly resemble divine Love. It's structurally impossible.

Yet the ability to briefly color that worldly love relationship with a pastel halo of blissful divinity, offers a hint about what's actually true in the Love department. Although we seek outwardly for love from others (with, uh, variable results), we carry within us the seed of potential to draw forth infinitely perfect divine Love from within our own being. Which is the only place it can truly be found.

So divine Love really is ours, in other words. It comes from no other place than within the self. And the magic that draws it out of hiding? An undefended heart. A completely wide-open, innocently un-armored heart sings at a joyous frequency that briefly touches the divine.

The following story illustrates such an appearance of divine Love, issuing forth from within:

In my senior year of high school, one day in the cafeteria while carrying my lunch tray back to my seat, I noticed a besotted boyfriend holding the hands of his comparatively noncommittal beloved across the lunch table.

He gazed dreamily into her eyes for a long while as I seated myself and began my meal. At last he spoke to her.

'I love you,' he fervently murmured, 'more than God loves Jesus.'

Which, one table over, caused Pepsi to suddenly exit my nose with a certain amount of force. The incident stuck in my mind for a number of reasons, as you can imagine. Here's a diary entry from around that time, in which I pondered the episode in more detail.

April 19, 1975
Apart from that bizarre statement (So wrong!! For so many reasons!!!!!!) something else was happening that I can't quite figure out. God Boy had some kind of religious glow about him. But Jesus Girl did not. He had this almost visible cloud of joy or something, streaming all around him. Sort of like he swallowed a flashlight made of happiness. She was just kind of sitting there. I'm not sure what the difference was. She's obviously into him. Who knows, maybe she even loves him. But if so, it's normal love. Regular person love. Not the happy-clappy-bright-and-shiny thing he has going on.

Inappropriate Sunday school weirdness aside, I realize now, that kid was actually onto something. There was indeed a divine aspect to his blissfully one-sided romance. As for me, I experienced my own glorious brush with the divine exactly once, a year or so after graduating from high school. And I never felt it again after that—at least, never again through worldly romance.

However the fact remains I did briefly experience capital 'L' Love while blissfully caught up in the throes of worldly first love. I didn't realize it back then, but there was no way this divine radiance could have been externally supplied by my much older (and recently divorced) boyfriend. His wounded heart was focused on other things. My own temporarily un-defended heart had been hoping for a duet, but in fact it sang solo. The radiant halo of Love I therefore experienced was un-questionably mine alone; true divine Love had come from no-where else but within me.

3. Light

Metaphysical teachings suggest spiritual Light exists on a con-tinuum. The same continuum, in fact, as regular visible light. Spiritual Light, they state, is simply much higher and finer in its vibratory frequency, and therefore beyond the compara-tively narrow slice of the spectrum visible to the physical eye, or measurable by instruments.

We know physical light provides one of the key building blocks of life on Earth, giving rise to functions like photosyn-thesis, as one example. Most living beings require the sun's light in one form or another, in order to thrive.

As we move higher up the frequency scale, capital 'L' Light reveals its more divine characteristics. (Or should I say, its more mysteriously esoteric characteristics.) Spiritual Light is a carrier of luminously divine information. Where shadows function always to shroud or fuzz out the truth, divine Light works in the opposite way. Its presence reveals clarity, truth and wisdom. Solutions to intractable problems effortlessly arise in divine Light's presence.

When we work intentionally with present moment Aware-ness, divine Light makes a mysterious guest appearance, joining seamlessly to function indivisibly as the radiant Light of Aware-

The Fricken Map is Upside Down

ness. The same thing happens with the magnificent Light of Love. We're not consciously asking for it in either case. Divine Light shows up entirely on its own, seemingly coming in from someplace else. Or at least that's how we tend to experience it.

The transcendent Light of infinite Source wisdom usually doesn't feel like an intrinsic part of our self. At least, not the self we're familiar with. Yet we know light, small 'l' light, is undeniably part and parcel of life on Earth. Why wouldn't the higher end of the same spectrum be an intrinsic part of our larger existence as well?

In fact it is. Or at least, it can be. When we consciously begin to work with present moment Awareness, it brings a corresponding rise in our overall degree of consciousness, which means our own energetic frequency rises as well. (Frequency and consciousness are inseparable. They rise or fall together.)

As our frequency rises, the higher, finer frequencies of Light naturally become more available to us. They're here all the time as part of the natural spectrum. Our own energetic frequencies just need to catch up a bit before most of us can experience this for ourselves.

Divine Light is our birthright. It isn't necessary to be able to see this Light with the inner eye, in order to derive its benefits. Some are talented in that way, some are not. But all of us can go within to experience its healing clarity and divinely illuminated wisdom. Even if we're seemingly doing it in the dark.

ATTITUDE ADJUSTMENTS

Following is a series of attitude adjustments I've chosen to make in recent years. I speak of them here before getting into any of the exercises, because I've found the journey flows infinitely faster and more enjoyably, now that my attitude is better aligned with the evolutionary process itself. Perhaps not all of them will apply to you. These are simply the attitudinal shifts I found helpful for my own journey. Take from them what you will.

1. A committed relationship with the self

As always, all of the exercises and meditations in this section presuppose an attitude of patience, acceptance, respect and non-judgment toward all parts of the self, no matter how far from the Light they may currently seem.

We are here as the compassionate witness, bringing the non-judging Light of divine Awareness to all of our explorations. We are never here to fix or heal. We are never here to get rid of anything; we couldn't if we tried. Accompanied by inner divine radiance, we are here to teach ourselves unconditional love for all parts of the self. And it's this unconditional love that leads us, slowly but surely, toward real divine Love for all. It's a process that brings miraculous transformation in its wake.

This does not happen overnight, nor does it happen in 'Point A to Point B' linear fashion. Or at least, it doesn't look quick or linear from within our skewed egoic perception. In fact, healing and evolution can unfold in ways that are breathtakingly quick, comparatively speaking, and stunningly direct. It just may not feel like it at the time.

It's worth noting you might not feel an attitude of genuine love, gratitude, respect or appreciation for your own deepest subterranean aspects right away. As you saw earlier, I certainly didn't. If that's the case, don't force it.

Just be honest with yourself, and start where you are. Set aside all you think you know about the egoic self, and regard it

The Fricken Map is Upside Down

as a blank slate. Be patient, be kind, and treat your own subterranean self like a foster kid who has arrived on your doorstep full of spiky, armor-plated attitude. It may be highly skeptical of your efforts at first.

You'll almost certainly make mistakes as you feel your way into a sincere relationship of deep and abiding mutual trust. Forgive yourself for your missteps. This foster kid, like anybody else, just wants to be loved. With your sincere ongoing efforts, the relationship with this seemingly separate part of your self will surely blossom in time.

It's this slow-built bond of authentic trust that allows the subterranean self to relax a bit, thereby creating space for the inner Light of divine wisdom to make its presence known. As all parts of the self begin to work together toward wholeness, you'll quickly discover divine liberation starts to unfold in ways both wondrous and unforeseen.

2. Making friends with the shadow

Like the relationship itself, this is a commitment that takes time to develop—but develop it must. In my experience, fearless embrace of the shadow aspect is a prerequisite for profound inner freedom. We must become willing to go absolutely anywhere, to witness and accept absolutely anything about ourselves.

As my 'twin' experience illustrated, this may include any unresolved ancestral or past life stuff stored in cellular memory that may still be impacting your ability to thrive in this present time. Even if you've never given much credence to the idea of cellular memory (or past lives, for that matter), do be kind to the ancient stuff that may or may not be lodged in those cells.

When the entire self is working together in partnership, the process itself is one of great gentleness and perfect timing. We don't do any of this alone, nor are we ever pushed to take on more than we can handle. Along the way, we learn to be relentlessly compassionate with whatever arises, embracing the subterranean shadow aspects even when we are triggered and don't feel like it.

Try to be patient and uncritical with yourself in this process, when you inevitably fall short of your own expectations. Fearless compassion toward all parts of the self includes you, and it doesn't necessarily come automatically. It's a learned process, and again, you start wherever you're at. As mutual trust grows, you get better at being there unconditionally for the entire self.

The 'foster kid with the bad attitude' may rebuff all our efforts at kindness at first. It sometimes seems to take a few months, before real trust is offered. But when the subterranean self finally decides our reconciliation efforts are indeed genuine, it meets us way more than halfway in that bond of mutual trust. And then, even when we do mess up or fall short, our failed efforts are still met with enormous gratitude that we've tried our best. Even if our best, in that particular moment, wasn't very good.

3. Why does spiritual progress have to be so hard?

It doesn't. It really, really, honest-to-God doesn't. This is, in many ways, the granddaddy of all the attitude adjustments. It seems simple, yet just about everything hinges on it.

For decades I assumed meaningful spiritual breakthrough could only occur through a hard-won hero's journey. Freedom should arrive reeking of sweat, triumphant at last over seemingly insurmountable inner and outer obstacles. (Swelling theme music optional.)

I didn't realize I felt that way. Often I tried to embrace the opposite approach, which seemed to actually work: More than once over the years, my desire for gentle progress would cause a deep karmic pattern to suddenly release, in a quick and unexpectedly easy way. But the requirement for hard-earned

The Fricken Map is Upside Down

freedom was a very firmly embedded belief, indeed. Each time a pattern released, the shift came so effortlessly that I couldn't trust it was real. I mean, dang, I hadn't even sweated a bit. This couldn't really be freedom.

Looking back, I now realize these patterns had indeed been released completely. But I couldn't accept freedom if the process didn't hurt. So the karmic pattern had no choice but to return—because I insisted it should.

I had to sit myself down in recent years and consciously undo my longstanding semi-unconscious beliefs about the necessity of doing it the hard way. For me, that gradual change included coming to know I deserved ease. In general, it's a great self-kindness to allow progress made with ease.

I mention all this, because spiritual alchemy happens quickly and easily, relatively speaking. Therefore I recommend looking carefully into your own beliefs, if you have not already done so, to make sure you're able to allow such ease. Make sure you know you're worthy of grace, whether you work hard for it or not. A clearly held belief that you deserve unobstructed ease and grace, can save lots of time and effort later on.

4. Notice the narrator

This one is primarily a reminder for vigilance. In your meditation explorations, be aware of the inner narrator, whose job is to speak words about your feelings, as a substitute for actually feeling them: *I allow this heart to open and receive!* is not even remotely the same thing as allowing this heart to open and receive.

Feeling our own authentic feelings is the only thing we ourselves can do that facilitates healing and evolution. To let the inner narrator speak words about a feeling state instead of daring to experience the feeling state itself, is like the difference between having our own basket of gold coins, or watching somebody else counting their gold coins.

And here's the attitude adjustment part of this reminder: The chatterbox narrator who accompanies our meditation is not evil. It's just trying to help, while maintaining safety and control of our experience in the only way it knows how. At times, its presence is even useful and needed—when stating an inner intention, for instance. *I allow this heart to open and receive!*, when followed up by actually allowing the heart to open and receive, is a beautiful thing.

As with any other aspect of the self that arises, train yourself to be relentlessly fond and patient with the narrator; its illusory existence is yet another invitation to be awestruck by the complex mystery that goes by the name of you. Just don't mistake its spoken declarations for your own authentic experience.

5. A balancing act

Ready access to divine wisdom and discernment is always required, in our explorations of subterranean secrets and shadows. A strong practice of resting in the present moment Light of Awareness, therefore, always accompanies our inward journeys into the shadow parts of the self.

Only divine wisdom can truly know when it's helpful to respect the privacy barriers of the subterranean self. Sometimes backing off really is the most loving and appropriate thing to do. Other times it's best to overlook an inner barrier, and compassionately bring the Light of divine Awareness inside—whether we have subterranean permission to enter or not. Only the divine self is capable of making this call.

It's also a good idea to always keep in mind that the nature and job description of the subterranean self is to supply us with distracting storylines to prolong our spiritual quest. Sometimes there are excellent reasons for that; sometimes not. A strong foundation in present moment Awareness will

The Fricken Map is Upside Down

help us discern when exploration of a storyline will lead ultimately to greater healing and freedom—or when it will lead to yet more loop-de-loops by the side of the road.

So what should our overall attitude be, when we're sometimes respecting its needs, yet at other times seemingly ignoring the subterranean self's wishes? Feeling good about the partnership is easy when we're giving the self what it's asking for. But in the beginning I felt guilty and apologetic when standing firm, as if I was betraying the subterranean self in my attempts to release it from its own self-made prison. That's not helpful. I've found it's better to think of the process this way:

It's like being the parent of a child with a debilitating illness. She is learning how to walk again. The physical therapy exercises hurt, sometimes more than others. The child often whimpers or cries. You, the loving parent, gently keep the exercises going. You do it because you know they will ultimately help this child be free. As you patiently lead her through her therapy exercises you hold the clear vision in your mind's eye, of this little one running joyfully through a golden meadow, with the sun on her face.

When the child cries out that the pain is too great, you stop and comfort her. Sometimes during this process you are urging the child forward. Other times you are resting with her patiently in divine solace until she is ready to try again. In every instance, your overall attitude never changes: The child is the Beloved.

Carrie Triffet

THE EXERCISES

Spiritual hygiene

These days I tend to begin each day's meditation by clearing my mind, body and field. This section begins with my favorite spiritual hygiene exercise, even though this meditation wouldn't ordinarily come first chronologically.

This exercise clears the mind, body and energetic field with a shower of divine Love-Light. The exercise gains its power from our faith or knowing (or delusional decision) that God is the only true power.

If you're not yet entirely convinced of this truth—and let's face it, most of us are not—you may wish to call in your 'spirit team' (everybody has one) and ask them to hold space for you during this exercise. They do know, without question or doubt, that God is the only power. Your team will therefore act as an amplifier and reflector of this cleansing Love-Light. The Love-Light is yours, available at your request. You're not asking 'outside' angels or guides to provide it. Your team is just here to support you, if you can't quite believe in your own ability, or right, to ask for and receive an omnipotent shower of Love-Light direct from your true Source.

As with any visualization exercise, it doesn't matter whether we're able to see the suggested images. What does matter is that we choose to believe the exercise is having real effects, whether we see the images or not. (It's yet another example of calculated delusionality: I'm supposed to be seeing divine Light right now. Do I see the divine Light? No I do not. I choose to believe divine Light is here anyway, operating at full capacity whether I'm experiencing it or not.)

Another way of saying this is, it isn't helpful to spend an entire meditation questioning whether we're doing it right.

The Fricken Map is Upside Down

That's just a spiritual way of beating ourselves up. If you're one of the many who are prone to this sort of behavior, please do yourself a favor. Decide you're doing it right. Decide you're always doing it right. Even if it turns out you really are doing it wrong, the journey will be way more fun and interesting while you're figuring it out.

EXERCISE

Breathe gently and naturally, following the rising and falling of the breath as it travels through the body. As you breathe, imagine you're sending roots of Light down from the soles of your feet, into the Earth. These roots are illuminated by the pure, concentrated power of divine truth. Feel the roots connecting you securely to the Earth.

Now focus within the heart space. Rest here in the heart, and call in your spirit team. Thank them for coming. (They're really here, whether you feel their presence or not.) Ask them to hold space, give support, amplify and reflect the divine Love-Light of Source, which you affirm is your true identity. Intend that this Love-Light takes the form of a softly rushing waterfall. Again, intention is all that matters here. Being able to see or feel the waterfall is optional.

Place yourself under the waterfall, open up and and let its sparkling pure 'waters' of Love-Light flow through all aspects of your mind, body and energy field. Intend that nothing can possibly resist the rushing downward flow of this beautiful waterfall. Silently state your intention that any form of energy out of alignment with your highest good is washed away now.

Imagine the rushing water easily carrying away all mental, physical and energetic debris. Imagine it all streaming out through the soles of the feet, into the roots of Light. As all the bits of gunk get washed away, bless and thank each one. Acknowledge its perfect role in helping you discover more of who you truly are. Wish it well on its recycling journey back to its Source.

Each bit of debris dissolves harmlessly as it moves out of the feet and through the roots of Light. Within these pure, concentrated roots of illuminated truth, shadowy misperceptions can't exist, so all debris is recognized as God, and dissolves effortlessly into the Light.

Now only Light and truth remain. Thank the Earth for its role in supporting and anchoring these roots of Light. Let the Earth itself be blessed and nourished by their divine radiance.

As you get used to doing this exercise, you'll find the waterfall cleanse itself can be quite brief. It only takes thirty seconds or so to bathe in this way, but it feels so refreshing you may want to stay longer. I would recommend doing this at least once a week, or even once a day wouldn't hurt. Until we're all ascended masters who only see pure divine truth everywhere we look, our minds, bodies and energy fields will continue to be affected by the world around us (because we'll believe they can). In the meantime, tools like this one are helpful.

Although this waterfall exercise is designed as an expedient tool of limited truth, it can grow and expand as we do. For me, the waterfall evolves continually. My desire is to erase all trace of enemy perception from my own mind, body and field. Therefore, as my own spiritual wisdom deepens over time, I've come to spend my waterfall interludes celebrating the God-perfection of all shadowy gunk everywhere. The gunk is fine. It's only me who hasn't quite viewed it correctly. So in my morning hygiene routine, as I stand beneath the perfect waterfall that I am, I ask only to cleanse my own perception.

*   *   *   *

On the subject of believing in the existence and power of one's own spirit team, I'll share a personal story here. If you're a chronic doubter about the existence, or maybe the commitment level of your own team, this story might provide a little food for thought:

Since early childhood when city blocks would rearrange themselves at will, I was terrified of getting lost. This fear was seamlessly

The Fricken Map is Upside Down

intertwined with the belief God had washed its hands of me, having abandoned me to the care of a cruel prankster universe instead.

As an adult, being lost always put me into bunny-in-the-headlights mode—a carefully managed state of quiet, controlled, grown-up panic, from which I did my best to access problem-solving logic. Over the years I learned to cope. I memorized landmarks; I navigated by the sun; I taught myself to read maps, and to negotiate California freeways.

Here in the English countryside it's a different story. All hedgerows look alike to me. Roads wind back on themselves. There are no street signs. I therefore tend to avoid driving anyplace new and unfamiliar, due to the dearth of recognizable landmarks and compass points. One day last year I decided to buck that trend, and arranged to meet a friend for coffee in a town an hour away. My GPS got me there without any problem.

After coffee we said our goodbyes at my car. As she walked away I started the engine and waited for the sat nav to find its satellites. And waited. And waited. And waited some more. The inspiration bubbled up then, to dig out my American phone (with its bigger screen than my UK phone) and use Google Maps instead.

Google Maps chose a route seemingly through northern France or someplace. Furthermore, it seemed to choose every damn single-track lane it could find. 'Single-track' means the road is the exact width of one vehicle. If you meet another, one of you needs to back up—sometimes uphill and around corners—until you find a spot to pull over. I am not a fan of single-track lanes. I go miles out of my way to avoid them.

A few minutes into this journey, the Nice Lady Google Voice suddenly stopped telling me what to do. Google Maps was still working, but silently. This meant I now had to keep one eye on the phone at all times, both for directions and to ensure the screen didn't go to sleep. The headlight bunny was still functioning, but she was a wee bit tense and shaky by this point.

After a half hour or so I couldn't help noticing I was being taken through the most gloriously scenic bits of countryside, now bathed in perfect, golden late afternoon sunlight. I also noticed I hadn't met even one oncoming vehicle in any of the single-track lanes. A flash of divine inspiration sparkled in: Maybe I could just enjoy the exquisitely beautiful journey itself, and let Google Maps (or perhaps my team) do the work. Bunny panic, it suggested delicately, was optional.

Okay, three things. One: There is no wifi in the countryside. Two: In many areas there is also no mobile phone coverage. Three: It was my *American phone*. It doesn't function here. In short, it is utterly impossible that Google Maps worked at all. Yet it did, seamlessly and without interruption.

Upon my safe arrival home, I sat down for a *what the hell just happened?* meditation. Although I had long accepted the idea my team is real, I had always believed I wasn't talented enough (or maybe special enough) to receive their support in actual, real-time daily life situations. They gathered for my meditations because I asked them to, I believed. But surely they wouldn't be paying attention throughout my day. Surely they were busier than that.

As I tuned in, I felt a general sort of celebration going on, a series of nonphysical high-fives. They were delighted I was getting the message: *We're real. We're here. We've got your back, in ways you've yet to imagine.*

I decided to be delusional from that point on, and simply know I'm supported by my team at all times, whether I feel their presence or not. The same, of course, is true for you.

One last point, about the existence of teams, angels, guides— or indeed any of the Nature figures and otherworldly beings I've spoken of in this book. Yes, these divine figures do exist (to the same degree anything else exists), and they agree to act as support figures within the game. They are radiantly Aware of their own divinity and ours. They're here to help until we fully recognize our own holiness, at which point we'll also recognize the divine gifts of wisdom, Love, safety and support they offer us are ultimately found only within.

In the meantime, our skewed egoic perceptual lens causes

The Fricken Map is Upside Down

us to perceive these figures and their extraordinary gifts as existing outside ourselves. This is how the subterranean lens functions; it's not so much that it acts as a fog obscuring true vision. It's a smashed perception, splintering our view of reality into seemingly separate, disconnected bits. To us, everything looks like endlessly shifting kaleidoscopic patterns, most of which seem to be occurring outside, not within.

Forgiveness and deep acceptance of our own self begins the process of healing the splintered vision. After I fully embraced the bad guy within, a flood of perceptual healing came in its wake. I no longer felt the need to disown and project outward that particular set of painful splinters; because of this I began to notice the kaleidoscopic programming itself dissipating at record speed. Now I find I'm increasingly noticing the divine attributes of otherworldly team figures are actually my own: My Love. My safety. My infinite wisdom and strength. But as of this writing, it's still a partial, splintered knowing. In the meantime I'm deeply grateful my team is here to help me, for as long as I seem to need the support.

A preliminary practice to develop Awareness

Your conscious focus is what automatically imbues Awareness with divine Light; Awareness becomes the Light of Awareness. To cultivate my own familiarity with the properties of Awareness, I found it helpful to give it a little bit of 'physical' space away from my own thinking mind. Try this exercise and see if it works for you.

EXERCISE

Sit comfortably somewhere in your home. Close your eyes, and place your Awareness inside a different room of your house, a room you know well. 'Look around' at the details of that space. This doesn't involve visualization talent. You're drawing on memory, here. Inhabit this other room with your full attention. Don't use your mind to think about the space. Practice simply being radiantly Aware of the details in the other room. Notice what radiant Awareness feels like.

Do this brief practice for at least a minute, a few times a day. You'll soon get good at recognizing the difference between your habitual mind and the more freely spacious and untethered state of radiant Awareness. And once that happens, you'll also understand how easy it is to shift between them.

Here's why this practice is fundamental. The habitual mental state is sort of like being a small kid enthralled with the Christmas window displays outside the local department store. You peer through the window and see magic, movement, color and fantasy. Never mind that it isn't real, and only exists to sell you stuff. The toy world it projects is mesmerizing. You are oblivious to all else.

Yet when the Light of Awareness causes you to temporarily refocus your eyes to the foreground, you see your own reflection in the glass instead. For the first time you notice with interest the frosty steam of your breath as it leaves your

The Fricken Map is Upside Down

mouth. You notice the texture of the knitted hat that's been keeping your ears warm all along.

Maybe you become aware of your feet, numb with cold on the frozen sidewalk. You've been standing motionless for such a long time, you now realize. Are they stuck to the pavement, you wonder? Experimentally you lift one foot and carefully set it down again. You try the other foot. As you observe all these newly remembered aspects of your self up close, the blur of fantasy movement in the background becomes far less believable (and far less desirable) as your only reality.

Learning to shift into radiant Awareness a few times a day helps to break our unquestioned hypnotic identification with the fantasy. Self-realization slowly starts to dawn as we come face to face, again and again, with our own remarkable reflection quietly looking back at us.

Carrie Triffet

BECOMING FAMILIAR WITH
THE PRESENT MOMENT

EXERCISE

1. Awareness in the present moment

Enter the spacious state of Awareness, just listening to your own breath and any sounds of life happening around you. Now focus the Light of your Awareness on the present moment. Quietly remind yourself that only this moment exists. Feel into the truth of this statement.

Notice any resistance that arises. If this particular now moment seems boring, disappointing, claustrophobic, or unsatisfactory in any way, hold all these uncomfortable feelings softly and steadily in your radiant Awareness.

Notice what the resistance (if any) feels like in your body. Notice you're still okay, even though discomfort may be happening. You are not the discomfort. Let all feelings be exactly as they are; just observe them with kindness and interest, while maintaining the state of present moment Awareness. Do this for at least a minute, or as long as you can hold the focus.

What you're doing is compassionately allowing the mind to express its fears, while becoming more comfortable with spending time in presence. Do this mini-meditation once a day until present moment resistance softens.

2. Present moment exploration inside the body

This meditation was pivotal for me. As I described earlier, it wasn't until I followed the inspiration to rest as present Awareness inside the body itself (as opposed to resting in the inner universe within) that I realized I had never actually inhabited my own body before. A surprising thing to discover!

The Fricken Map is Upside Down

I include this fairly advanced meditation in this early section, simply because it fits the overall present Awareness theme. But I'll point out once again I was only guided to try this meditation after I'd already stopped wanting to harbor the dark secrets I was carrying in cellular memory. In this sort of meditation the body-mind is given nowhere to hide. Had I still been strongly embracing a need for shadows, this would have been a very uncomfortable and unkind exercise to inflict upon the subterranean self.

Yet instead of discomfort, it felt refreshingly healthy. And sane (meaning un-splintered) in a way I'd never known. It felt so good to experience my mind, body and conscious Awareness all agreeing to show up in the same moment, the same place, and same dimensional timeline. The difference was eye opening.

I doubt I'm alone in my lifelong refusal to inhabit my own body in the now moment. Likewise, I have no doubt many shadowy beliefs are held in almost everybody's cellular memory. So if you find this exercise brings any kind of serious resistance from your own mind and body, do be kind.

Back off and make a date instead to explore the body-mind's hidden cellular secrets at some other more appropriate time. And then come back to this exercise when all parts of you are more ready and willing to experience your body-mind here, now, in the sparkling beauty of the present moment.

EXERCISE

Take your radiant Awareness inside the physical body. As the present-moment Light of Awareness, rest inside the body and simply breathe. Be the witness inside your body. Explore. See what it feels like to rest within the lungs; the stomach; the heart. Rest inside bone. Go wherever the body calls your attention.

Explore what it's like to fully be here, now, in this body in this moment. Breathe.

Acknowledge divinity is present in this moment. Love is present in this moment.

Can you be here where your body is, without mental or physical resistance? Can you allow the divine Light of Love to be present while you do this?

What does it feel like to inhabit your own body, right now, knowing that divinity is present here too? Witness the whole self, to the best of your ability, in the Love and Light of divine Awareness.

If anything specific arises to be looked at, just witness it with the Love and Light of divine Awareness. Transmit the message and feeling to all of the body's cells: It is SAFE to be here now inside this body.

SOURCE MEDITATIONS

The following Source meditations were some of the earliest exercises I was given. They were from a time when I could not yet feel the truth of my own Source divinity within. Although I clearly understood that all is God, and divinity is found only within, this understanding was not reflective of my actual experience.

My own mind, body and energy field still felt very separate from our shared Source. These exercises were therefore designed to help the mind, body and field get used to 'Source proximity,' so to speak.

As always, if your mind or body objects strongly to an exercise, respect the feedback and back off. Always be patient and kind with the self. No doubt the subterranean self has very good reasons for its objections!

1. Filling the body's cells with Source

Sink into the present moment Light of Awareness, and go inside the physical body.

Witness the body as being made up of all its cells. Quietly place your conscious Awareness inside all the cells of the body. (This is accomplished merely through your stated intention.) Do this very gently, as the cells are not accustomed, at first, to being the subjects of conscious attention. Just observe.

Then, if it feels appropriate, softly allow your Source to fill all your cells to the brim. Rest here, allowing all your cells to marinate in their Source.

2. Filling the mind with Source

Move into the radiant Light of Awareness, and bring your focus inside the head. Rest there. Open and relax all brain function, all thought patterns, and every aspect of the mind. Relax all memory. Relax all mental beliefs. Relax the narrator.

Witness the entire mind with (and as) the compassionate Light of Awareness. Rest as this neutral witness.

If it feels appropriate, let all parts of the mind be filled with their Source. Resist nothing, and rest the entire mental body in Source.

3. Filling the central column with Source

Sink into the divine Light of present moment Awareness, and bring your focus within, to the central core of the inner energetic body. Here there is a vertical column of pure divine Light. Rest your Awareness inside this central column of Light. (It isn't important to be able to see the column of Light. Just intend to be inside it.) Explore in here.

How does it feel to bring your conscious Awareness inside this repository of your own perfect divinity? Feel into recognizing this column of divine Light as your own identity. Can you feel yourself as this, even dimly?

If it feels appropriate, consciously invite your Source to be here with you. Let your central column of Light merge with its Source, until this column is completely filled up with Source. Rest inside here, with your own indwelling divinity merged with its pure Source.

The Fricken Map is Upside Down

4. Seeing a problem as God

Take the Light of Awareness into your inner space. Rest here. Now allow (intend) the body, mind and energy field to fill with radiant Source presence.

If you have a physical issue, an emotional issue or other external problem, bring it into your radiant Awareness now. Witness it without judgment, and let it, too, fill with Source Light presence.

Feel into the truth: There is no difference between the Source Light that you are, and the Source Light that this issue is. All is God. This issue is God. Notice you haven't recognized this problem's true identity until now; you've been covering it over with your own Etch-A-Sketch doodles, your own beliefs and opinions about it.

Release your opinions and ideas about your issue. Give them back to Source. Rest together with the blank slate of this issue, in the pure divine Light of your Source.

About this meditation:
As we talked about earlier, Love-Light-Awareness is the only possible raw material for all of creation. Not only is Love-Light-Awareness the raw material, it is also the end product. It is God expressing as that. We are never required to like it. Our only job is to recognize and honor its true divine identity.

I can't stress it enough: This is a master key that unlocks all doors. When we recognize the real raw material and true identity of whoever or whatever is causing us upset, it not only frees us, it energizes that thing with the possibility of realigning in a way that better expresses its true divine identity. Mountains are moved when we make a habit of recognizing true identity. This exercise is a potent way to get that ball rolling.

EXPLORATIONS

1. Truth and untruth in the present moment

This exercise is a clear and useful illustration of the difference between two opposing ways of perceiving. It also makes clear that all problems are purely optional ideas. They're not rock solid truths.

EXERCISE

Move into the spacious Light of Awareness. Notice you are this radiant Awareness itself. Now feel into the present moment. Relax your Awareness, as deeply as you can, in the now. Rest here.

Notice there is no history here, and no future to be anxious about. Notice there are no problems in present moment Awareness.

Experiment with being absolutely fine with this moment. Feel what that's like.

Now stay firmly rooted in radiant Awareness and presence, but allow the mind back in, to remind you of what is not yet perfect about this moment. Let it list its problems, its worries and its unfinished business. As the Aware witness, notice the energy you spend resisting everything that is wrong with your life.

Toggle back to the way radiant Awareness witnesses this same moment. Notice how the energy spent on resistance contrasts with what it feels like to be fine in the present moment. Notice the choice is yours.

2. Investigation of the mind

Move into the radiant Light of present moment Awareness. Rest here in silence.

Now bring your Awareness inside the thinking mind itself. Let mental activity come and go as it pleases. But consciously notice every thought that arises.

Be the neutral, Aware witness, as you give full attention to your own mental activity. Let every thought and every idea without exception be illuminated by the conscious Light of Awareness.

Illumination simply means witnessing with the Lights turned on. No judgments are formed, no conclusions reached. No new 'facts' are presented to alter the story as you understand it to be. There is only witnessing in the presence of divine Light.

3. Yes, but

This luminous now moment only looks disappointing or unsatisfactory because we see it through the lens of the subterranean self, whose job description is, in part, to resist what is. By consciously stepping back from that lens, the sparkling purity and perfection of God-Creator-Source shines as our daily life at this moment—regardless of what the moment itself seems to hold.

Any moment will do, to experience this recognition of divine perfection. Every moment has it. And no moment will ever look like it has it, if that moment is viewed through our personal self's lens of judgment. So every moment is a good time for recognizing God perfection, and no moment will ever seem the right one.

Subterranean resistance is another way of saying, 'I believe in enemies.' To resist anything is to make an enemy of it. Our resistance offers much-needed food to the thing we resist. If we were to stop resisting it, the thing would lose momentum because its power depends upon the focused attention we nourish it with.

More important, to resist anything is to damn it as being separate and outside of God—which is a recipe for self-damnation. By continuously resisting what is, the subterranean self is a courageous volunteer for ongoing self-damnation.

It's the only way that you, the tip of the iceberg, get to experience yourself as a separate individual outside of all-that-is. All of you deserves to be freed from the pain of self-damnation. Every bit of you deserves to be lifted gently by your own higher aspects, and held and cherished as the miraculous offspring of the divine that you are. You, the conscious tip of the submerged iceberg, are the only one who can get this party started. Do it for all parts of the God self that you are in truth.

The following exercise is a deeper exploration of how the subterranean self interacts with the present moment. Its purpose is to help you investigate the subtler levels of background resistance to what is.

EXERCISE

Go within. Move gently into the present moment, in the Light of Awareness. Quietly feel into this moment's inherent perfection as it is right now. Rest here. If the subterranean self feels relatively comfortable to be here, now, as you witness the present moment in this illuminated way, see if you can tune into the self even more deeply.

In its agreement to be here, now, in this meditation, it is expressing a surface-level acceptance of the present moment. Look deeper. Can you pinpoint any subtle background resistance it may be feeling, to this illuminated now moment? See if you can locate 'yes, but.'

If you find it, ask respectfully to be allowed inside. Sit quietly within 'yes, but.' Look around. Be curious to find out what's living in here. Remember, we're here just to explore. Not to judge or change anything.

Notice if there's any physical resistance hiding within 'yes, but.' Is there a tightening in the belly? If so, go there gently and compassionately. Rest quietly inside that area of the body and be present with the discomfort.

If any physical feelings inside 'yes, but' are more extreme (headache, nausea, muscle cramps) back off immediately. Apologize to the subterranean self for the violation, and assure it that it is perfect as it is.

Apologize to the body, too. Its cells are crying out—they're

The Fricken Map is Upside Down

letting you know this exploration brings too much divine Light for them to metabolize, at this point in their evolution. Right now they're still carrying unconscious investment in darkness.

Always respect the self. Also make sure you're not bullshitting when you reassure it. Only speak what you feel in your heart. The self is you, it knows when you're lying.

If you've been allowed to explore inside 'yes, but' with minimal agitation or interference, flood this subtle background aspect of the self with all the acceptance, love and gratitude you can muster. Witness it in the clear-eyed Light of Awareness, and affirm its inherent right to be. Welcome 'yes, but.' Welcome every part of the inconvenient inner self. This is what sets the stage for magic and miracles.

When the self genuinely knows it is loved and appreciated for being exactly what it is, the now moment becomes far less terrifying. Far more approachable. And because of this, the inherent perfection of this now moment starts to reveal itself within the mundane chaos of our own daily existence.

And *then* we are able to dip a toe, and experience our first tentative droplets of Life lived brilliantly: The now-moment-by-now-moment flow of Life's majestic river, joyfully beckoning us to join in its irrepressible surge.

BEYOND THE 'I' SELF

1. Stepping outside the me-centric viewpoint

Some would say this meditation constitutes the truest form of prayer. With total openness and humility, our conscious Awareness rests silently in our Source. Divine Source is free to make itself known (or as free as we can allow) without being drowned out by the endless chatter of the thinking mind. We're not here to ask for anything. We simply rest and listen.

I found this meditation very freeing when it was first given to me. Although I loved working with it, I didn't fully appreciate at the time just how important this practice was to my evolutionary process. Looking back I later realized it was a key first step in allowing the Light of divine Awareness to flourish within my own consciousness: The divine self *as* me.

EXERCISE

Sink into the present moment Light of Awareness, and go within. Fill the body, mind and energy field with Source presence.

In the holy presence of your Source, do the following to the best of your ability: Experiment with stepping outside all sense of your own personal needs and wants.

Leave behind all thoughts of unfinished or unsatisfying life circumstances. Try being only the Aware witness of this moment. Rest in your Source as this impartial and uncluttered witness. Listen. Breathe. Be.

2. Detaching from the personal 'me'

The following exercise of stepping away from the personal self is a keystone practice for inner freedom. Its aims are different from those of the previous exercise. It's also different from a practice of resting as Awareness.

This one, the relinquishment of the personal perceptual lens, means we have no idea who or what we are. We're not placing our attention on our own existence; instead we rest as existence itself, having no backstory. No problems. No opinions. Nothing we're looking forward to. Our own needs (if we had any) would be seen as no more or less important than anybody else's.

Stepping away from personal perception, even for just five minutes, requires great trust between all parts of the self—for very obvious reasons. Don't underestimate the degree of bravery and selflessness it takes for the subterranean self to allow this exercise. One of these days, this practice or something like it, will help overturn its seemingly independent life within us. Naturally it wants to survive as much as we do. Maybe more.

So this is the greatest gift the subterranean self can offer us, and should never be taken lightly. To even try this exercise, the self must absolutely know we're not trying to kill it or abandon it. In the early days of preparing to do this exercise, I would first gather up all the aspects of me in a preliminary meditation and hold them close, filled with genuine love and admiration for them. Then together we would reach a consensus agreement to be homeless for a while.

It's a wonderful exercise for so many reasons. If you've always disliked your physical body (as I had) it's an amazing gift to simply be able to offer your Aware witness to each aspect of the physical self. There's no accompanying baggage, no opinions or judgment, no history of shame, no distaste—only spacious, effortless noticing of what's here. When I first tried it, it was a revelation, a startling window into a completely different way of relating to my own physical existence.

If you have chronic physical health challenges, you can go inside the body and do the same. You'll be astonished by the complete removal of your limiting, debilitating lens—and by how good that feels. No stories, no roadblocks, no assumptions that it's always been this way, therefore it always will. No assumptions of any kind. Just gently interested witnessing without personal attachment.

Carrie Triffet

When this skill is mastered, the same exercise becomes an invaluable tool for dealing with worldly issues as well. Before taking any action on a personal hotbutton issue, we can try going into this space of egoic 'homelessness' first. We can then perceive our issue without the entirely subjective Etch-A-Sketch scribbles we have innocently and unknowingly scrawled all over it in the past. We will see the situation as it really is, and it will look entirely different from the way it looked before. And from there, appropriate action can be taken as needed.

EXERCISE

We begin by holding the whole self in love and gratitude. We ask permission of all parts of the self: Can we temporarily step outside our own conscious lens of perception? If the answer is 'yes,' we move into the luminous state of Awareness, as we normally might. But now the Light of Awareness itself turns to 'look back' at the physical-mental-emotional-energetic self, and subtly detaches from it. We are the Awareness that looks back. Not the figure who sits in meditation.

This focus is held until the physical-mental-emotional-energetic 'you' is seen as being no more personal or important than a stranger walking by. Nothing is known about 'you.' Not even your name. You're like that little gray, silhouetted head that shows up in your favorite online app, when you've neglected to upload a profile photo. 'You' is a blank, generic question mark of a person. Rest with this unknowing.

This itself can be the full extent of the meditation. Or, as mentioned above, it can be the jumping off point to explore the so-called facts of your existence from this entirely new and liberating perspective.

The Fricken Map is Upside Down

RESTING IN THE LIGHT OF LOVE

Because I came into this life with a heavily defended heart, I was not naturally resonant to divine Love. I therefore tended to shy away from spiritual practices that made divine Love their principal focus, because I couldn't feel it.

I was convinced, down in those dark and distant parts of the self, that I would never be capable of feeling divine Love because I was made of something different. Something unholy and profane. And no amount of spiritual work on my 'surface half-acre of garden' seemed to alter those secret beliefs in any way.

Only with the practices outlined in this book has fundamental change occurred on the deepest, most otherwise-unreachable levels of the iceberg. That I now know myself as the Beloved, is but one benchmark of this profound shift.

1. The Light of Love as your own identity

Move into the radiant Light of present moment Awareness, and bring your focus into the heart space.

Feel into the soft Light of Love that is always present in you. (If you can't yet feel it, just peacefully know it's here, whether you can connect with it right now or not.) Rest here.

See if you can recognize the Light of Love as your own identity. Hold this focus of inquiry. See if, even faintly, you can begin to feel the soothing gentleness (a hallmark of divine Love) throughout your body, mind and energy field.

Allow the possibility that this is really true, whether you are able to feel it yet for yourself or not. Rest in the (aspirational) truth: The Light of Love is my true identity.

Carrie Triffet

2. Resting as the universal heart

Sink into the Light of spacious Awareness, and go within your own heart space. Imagine or feel that your heart space is the core of the universal heart. Move deep into the core of this vast heart, and rest here.

If it feels appropriate, release all personal barriers that would keep your heart separate; your heart and the universal heart are one.

Feel or imagine the delicate, yet powerful Love-Light radiating from the center of your heart. Let it mingle seamlessly with divine universal Love-Light, until only the universal heart (which also contains yours) remains. Experiment with feeling into this universal heart as your own Love-Light identity.

The Fricken Map is Upside Down

ROSE-GOLD MEDITATIONS

Let's talk about this rose-gold thing for a minute. The color I describe as the rose-gold Light of the unified masculine-feminine Christ, shows up for me as something like the delicate pink tinge of rose-gold metal: A perfect blend of soft white-gold and palest pink.

Or maybe it's more like the whisper-pale translucence of a dry rosé champagne. That's the sort of supremely delicate pinky-golden tone I'm talking about. But you might not see it as any specific color at all. The important thing is to feel into the nurturing frequency the rose-gold color emits, if you can.

1. Resting as rose-gold divinity

EXERCISE

Close your eyes and sink into the Light of present moment Awareness. Go within.

Imagine or feel that a soft rose-golden ball of Love-Light exists in the core of your being. It is goodness itself. Its presence is a gift. There is nothing difficult or challenging about it. Feel into the gentle, healing, reassuring rays of rose-gold Love-Light that it emanates.

Sink into this rosy-golden ball of Love-Light, and rest here. You deserve it. Allow every cell of the body to be nourished. Let its rose-gold goodness soothe every bit of the energy field. Everything about rose-gold is safe and welcoming for every part of you.

Experiment with feeling into this emanation, to see if you can find an inkling of your own rose-gold Love-Light identity in it. Can you feel any aspect of 'you' here?

Rest now, and surrender the body-mind-energy field to the soft, rose-gold Light of divinity that you are.

2. Rose-gold appreciation for what you are

This meditation cultivates deep appreciation for the truly wondrous and mysterious self, including the limited subterranean self we know ourselves to be. I've been talking throughout this book about the mysterious magnificence of what we all are. In this meditation I was able to experience it so much more profoundly than I ever had before—and I can only say our mind-blowing beauty, even as we are right now, is an experience not to be missed.

It came to me this way: One morning in meditation I began, as I often do, by resting as the rose-gold Light of Awareness. And then I peeled off into a little random daydream of some kind. As soon as I noticed, I brought myself back.

I'd always thought I was being kind yet firm, when catching that daydreaming part of the self. But this time I noticed I'd always applied very subtle judgment against that 'misbehaving' part of the mind—the underlying assumption being that daydreams are bad and meditations are good. In truth, such judgments are meaningless. The enemy daydreamer and the judgey meditator are both the same self.

This time I was suddenly seeing differently. This time I beheld all parts of the self from outside the lens of enemy consciousness. There was no judge present at all, toward the daydreamer or anybody else. And without the influence of a painfully judgmental lens, I was gob-smacked by the immense beauty and mysterious wonder of this egoic self. *Incredible,* I thought. *How amazing that I never noticed before.*

How magnificent, this ability to daydream! How breathtakingly complex, these multi-dimensional forays into past memory and future fantasy. This mind's vast web of connection to countless lifetimes and infinite dimensional timeline possibilities. This energetic body with its shared morphic fields, trading constant (mostly unconscious) information with other beings everywhere. This grand electromagnetic push-pull game of moment-by-moment reality simulation. What stunning creatures we are.

And this physical body! This cellular structure, this heart-beat, this breath. This evolving DNA, these intelligent genetic codes. I saw so clearly the exquisite divine identity of all these ingenious creations. They all seem to blot out our firsthand knowing of God, yes. They tend to promote suffering as a result. All games aside, I don't know why that is. I don't know what it's all for.

Nevertheless these structures themselves are gloriously and unmistakably divine. They are also inextricably part and parcel of the higher mind, the higher divine self; I saw and felt that clearly as well. Although they appear to be separate, it's all one continuous self—indivisible. How could it be other? And seeing this brought me such joy of recognition. And such deep appreciation for what I am. What we are.

We're like snowflakes, you and I, each of us uniquely complex and beautiful. No two exactly alike. We all fall from the clouds together, through some kind of prearranged collective decision. Gravity and weather patterns determine the shifting nature of our free-fall snowy descent. Sometimes it's gentle, slow, silent. Other times fierce, sideways and brutal. And as we all prepare to touch down and join those who've flurried in before us, every once in a while a snowflake lands instead on the waiting, outstretched tongue of God and dissolves instantly.

God claps its be-mittened hands in delight. To God, all snowflakes taste equally pure. Equally delicious. To the snowflake, now melted into warm liquid merged seamlessly in God, Life bursts with unexpected joy. It knows itself to be part of God now. It recognizes itself as perfect.

But it was always perfect, and it was always part of God. The snowflake was perfect while its crystals were forming. It was perfect as it fell. And it's perfect now, albeit in a different molecular state than it ever anticipated.

All is well, in other words.

All is always well, no matter how anything seems.

We need not wait until divinity catches us on its tongue (so to speak), to discover deep appreciation and awe for what we are. Try this exercise and see if you can get in touch with your own divine magnificence, your own truly awesome nature. Exactly as you are right now.

EXERCISE

Go into the inner heart space and rest as the radiant Light of divine Awareness.

Next, move your Awareness outside the body. Go across the room and look back at yourself, dis-identifying with the one who sits in meditation. Rest in this way.

Now (without moving your physical body) take your Awareness out of doors. Rest as Awareness inside a tree, and see if you can feel a glimpse of what it's like to be that tree, instead of being the one who sits in meditation. Do the same with a cloud, a chimney, a bird or whatever you choose. Rest as each of these things, and let your Awareness explore what it's like to be this thing or that creature. Try to feel into its perspective instead of your own.

Now bring your Awareness back into your own inner heart space. Allow it to come to rest on the altar of rose-gold divinity that is always already present here.

From this vantage point, turn once again, with neutral non-attachment, to witness the self who meditates. Ask the Love-Light of rose-gold divinity to illuminate this whole self so you, as Awareness, can witness it more clearly. Forget all you think you know about the self as you currently perceive it. Ask only to see the whole self, exactly as it is right now. As it truly is.

Rest in whatever arises as a response. And allow appreciation for whatever you are, for all that you are, to well up spontaneously and naturally from within. Rest in appreciation.

The Fricken Map is Upside Down

3. Rose-gold chakra meditation

The chakra system is found in the vertical central core of the energy body. When the whole energetic system is free of distortion and functioning perfectly, you would know your own divine multidimensional identity, and everybody else's, too. Yet all manner of unhelpful stuff accumulated throughout lifetimes typically causes these energy centers to operate with less than optimal efficiency.

The following rose-gold tour through the chakra system is a fairly advanced meditation, requiring full cooperation from all parts of the self. As you move through the chakras in this meditation, be very kind, patient and attentive to the whole self. Notice at every stage how all parts of the inner self may be responding to this work, and don't force it if you sense growing discomfort. This is a truly wonderful and powerful meditation—but only if you're not experiencing battles for control, or frightened subterranean efforts to protect secret shadows.

Remember, from their perspective, they have excellent reasons for fearing the Light. If one or more chakras refuse to let your Light enter, be patient and respectful. Go away and do more inner work to deepen your trust and love for all parts of the self, and then periodically, maybe every month or so, come back and ask permission to try this meditation again. It's worth the wait.

MEDITATION

Go within the inner space of the heart-solar plexus region, and rest as Awareness in the rose-gold Love-Light that you are.

Bring this rose-gold Love-Light of Awareness to the crown chakra at the top of the head. Rest as divine Love-Light inside this chakra.

Set aside all you think you know about this chakra. Let it be a blank slate, quietly bathing in Love-Light. Surrender control of this chakra to rose-gold divinity. Let there be no difference between your rose-gold Love-Light and the perfect true identity of this chakra.

Remind yourself that nothing is more powerful than God. Allow the rose-gold Love-Light that you are to witness any of this chakra's beliefs, blocks, distortions or hindrances as they truly are. You don't need to know the nature of these blockages.

If you receive information about a particular blockage, simply witness that information, holding it gently along with the blockage itself, in the rose-gold Love-Light of Awareness. Breathe.

Let the true God identity of this chakra and its blockages be revealed as parts of the same one divine identity. Let all blockages reveal to you they are made of God. And as they are recognized as this, let them be blessed and released harmlessly to reunion with all-that-is.

Give this chakra permission to function perfectly, according to its true nature. Rest within this pristine energy center, as the rose-gold Love-Light that you are. Rest as the divine recognizing the divine.

Repeat in descending order with the other six physical chakras: Third Eye, Throat, Heart, Solar Plexus, Sacral and Root Chakras, respectively, plus the Earth Star chakra located twelve inches or so below the feet. (I asked whether to include the trans-personal chakras above the head, but was given to understand this exercise isn't necessary for them, because they carry no density of forgetfulness regarding true identity. Include those energy centers if you want to, but it isn't required.)

4. Surrendering all to the rose-gold Light of divine Source

EXERCISE

Enter into the spacious Light of Awareness and rest here for a minute or two, listening to your own breath. Focus your

Awareness on the inner heart space. Rest all that you are on the altar of rose-gold divinity, and continue listening to your own breath.

Surrender the breath, allowing rose-gold divinity to take it over and be in charge of breathing. Feel this divine energy as it moves into the breath itself. It is trustworthy. Rest in rose-gold breath, secure in the knowledge that all is well.

Next surrender the heartbeat. Let rose-gold divinity take it over and be in charge of beating your heart. Feel the divine energy as it takes over this function. Know it is trustworthy. Rest in the rose-gold beating of your own heart. This job is no longer yours.

Then surrender the original spark of existence that you are. Visualize returning your spark of original conscious existence, your 'I am' spark of Light, to the soft, Loving 'parent' flame of infinite divinity. Let your 'I am' melt into the greater 'I am.' This is completely safe to do. The 'parent' flame of God is trust-worthy. *All is well.* Rest here, in gentle rose-gold union with the infinite Light of divine Source.

THE JOINING POOL

This exercise has been with me ever since the higher self first suggested it in 2011. Versions of it have appeared in two of my earlier books. As it continues to evolve, the pool remains surprisingly fresh and relevant even today.

The joining pool first appeared as a visualization tool for helping me (and others) counteract our strong egoic belief in separation. My mind did not welcome joining at first. The very idea felt like sandpaper scraping against my brain. Yet with a little practice, joining became a beautiful, enjoyable activity. The following is the original joining pool exercise as it first appeared.

1. Original joining pool exercise

Go within, to the inner heart space. Visualize a circular cavern here. It's large and clean and airy feeling. A sparkling pool of water is found at the center of the cavern. That pool of water is your Source, and it's infinitely deep.

If you've brought specific worries into this cavern with you, you can leave them by the side of the pool; there's no need to bring them beyond this point. Your Source knows what all your illusory troubles are. You're free to release them now.

Dive into the pool. As you do so, intend that your body is water-soluble. Feel the cells of your bones, muscles, organs and skin filling with water and gradually dissolving away until only your thinking mind and Awareness remain.

Now relax the boundaries of your thinking mind. Let its edges soften, visualizing the water as it gently fills up the thinking mind and slowly dissolves it as well.

Now you're nothing but pure Awareness. Let your Awareness lose all characteristics of individuality, merging completely with the perfect water. Stay in this formless state for as long as possible.

It was suggested to me in 2014, that I should try to feel into the idea that *I am* the joining pool. The pool was not something separately perfect and pristinely divine that I was merging into, in other words—I was the divine pool as well as the self-limiting human who was performing the joining exercise.

At the time I did my best to experience this fairly mind-blowing suggestion, in a nervously peek-a-boo, *Who, little ol' me?* sort of way. Now, years later, this recognition of *I am* identity (while still incomplete) is fundamental to my daily experience. But back then a joining pool made of the divine water that I am, was my first hands-on introduction to my own true nature.

2. The waterfall

I don't really know why I stopped working with the joining pool. I guess it no longer seemed relevant. Picking it back up within the past year, I saw it was still a great exercise exactly as it was first conceived. But its thrilling possibilities and rapid evolutionary pace really took off with the introduction of rose-gold Light.

For this next exercise my joining pool spontaneously relocated itself outdoors into sparkling sunlight. Feel free to keep your pool in the safety of the cavern if that feels right.

In this exercise the joining pool itself remains as it always has been, but now at one end is a majestic waterfall. (Yes, it's the same waterfall as the one in the hygiene exercise.) The water is made entirely of the pristine diamond Light of Source. This is pure, sparkling divine power, flowing over you, through you and as you. It is gentle and refreshing. I picture myself standing under it, and feeling the wonderful cleansing flow. I let its healing water penetrate every cell of my body, mind and energy field. As best I can, I feel into its true identity as being inseparable from my own.

The point here is not so much the clearing of unwanted debris, as the attempt to recognize one's own divine identity is one and the same as that of the water. This exercise is therefore useful in strengthening the recognition that God is the only true power. As in the hygiene exercise, the waterfall's emphatic downward flow helped me believe in its divine ability to wash away all foggy misperception that seems to stand in the way of God recognition.

The rushing water is not making an enemy of anything. From the divine water's perspective, it joyously reunites with the unwanted veils and misperceptions; the water knows their true divine identity, even when I did not. My job was only to offer gratitude for their being, as the unwanted misperceptions were gently made transparent to the Light, and then released.

3. The rose-gold mist

The waterfall has a magnificent, beautiful mist rising off it. This exquisitely soft mist is the rose-gold Light of divinity. The mist nurtures, heals and soothes. It is pure solace when life hurts. It is pure joy when it doesn't. I would often bring the subterranean self here whenever it was having a hard time with the pace of evolution. We would rest quietly together, drinking in the pure, wordless compassion of delicate rose-gold divinity.

Other times I would simply choose to rest here at the start of my morning meditation. There are few nicer ways to begin the day.

4. The rose-gold pool

Have I mentioned the pool itself turned rose-gold? Spectacular. It happened only a few months after the arrival of the waterfall and its rose-gold mist. The rose-gold pool embodies not only the divine attributes of the joining pool (no small thing!), but also the perfectly balanced and unified masculine-feminine Christ energies in all their glory.

This rose-gold pool is far more wondrous than the mind can grasp. I myself perceive its vastness, power and infinite goodness only dimly. Here are just a few of its attributes:

* The rose-gold pool is completely customized and specific to each individual's journey, offering just the right form of help for that person in any given moment.

* The pool acts as a bridge between 3D physicality and the etheric body, effortlessly accessing all dimensions and time lines to reach every part of the multi-dimensional self. It also accesses all parts of the unconscious iceberg. No part of the self is unreachable, in other words, in the rose-gold pool.

* The pool acts to focus and amplify our stated intentions and prayers, simultaneously purifying them (and us!) for the highest good.

These days I rarely spend time in the exquisitely delicate mist anymore, preferring to soak in the soothing full-body bliss of rose-gold splendor instead. See if you agree. Spend some time getting to know the mist, allowing your mind, body and energy field to slowly acclimate to its sweet, healing frequencies. Then take a dip in the pool and receive its full rose-gold expression. You might never go back.

Carrie Triffet

5. Rose-gold breath

Rose-gold breath is not a breathing practice per se; the breath remains completely unforced and natural. We just intend that the breath's identity is rose-gold, and we follow it mindfully through every inhale and exhale. It sounds simple (and it is) but the effects are profound.

EXERCISE

Bring your radiant Awareness into the rose-gold pool and rest here in presence. Let your Awareness softly merge with the pool itself.

Breathe naturally, *as* the rose-gold pool of Awareness. Focus your Aware attention on your own rose-gold breath as it rises and falls. Do this for as long as you like.

6. The rose-gold breath of Love

Because the resonance of divine Love was still a bit new and unfamiliar to me, compared with that of my old friends Light and Awareness, inspiration suggested I practice feeling into the divine identity of the pool as being pure, infinite Love. It took some concentration at first, and a few well-placed sparkles of calculated delusion, before I reliably felt the truth of rose-gold Love firsthand. Once that was accomplished, it was suggested I find my own I-am-the-pool identity as that same Love. Again, it took a bit of concentrated effort to feel myself as the divine Love identity of the rose-gold pool.

As soon as I did it, the pool became an infinite ocean. Dimly I recognized it as my own identity of endless Love. All on its own, the rose-gold breath became the rose-gold breath of Love, breathed now by the heart as well as the lungs. This breath of Love became the breath I used to bless the world, from that point on.

Bring your Light of Awareness into the rose-gold pool, merging your Awareness with the rose-gold pool itself. Breathe naturally, as the rose-gold pool of Awareness. Focus on this rose-gold breath as it rises and falls.

Feel into the true identity of this pool as being pure divine Love. Take as long as you need; employ a little bit of delusion if required. Breathe this divine Love for as long as you like. Breathe it through people or circumstances (or the world itself), eyes open or closed, as you feel inspired.

(Bonus round)
If appropriate, feel into your own identity as being one and the same as the rose-gold pool of divine Love. Let the pool-that-you-are expand into an infinite ocean. If it feels right, let the heart itself take over the act of breathing. Let the heart breathe you as an infinite ocean of Love. Use this Love breath to bless all.

7. The river of Life

And here is the river of Life exercise as I first received it. I can't recommend it highly enough.

EXERCISE

As the spacious Light of Awareness, enter the rose-gold pool. Drop inside the physical body. Feel your own breath as it enters and exits the lungs. In the safety of this sacred pool, tune in as deeply as you can to your own present-moment physicality. Rest here.

Let the physical self dissolve and merge with the pool. Notice the rose-gold pool is your own true divine identity. (You may or may not be able to connect with that truth firsthand. Allow it to be so, anyway.)

Now imagine the pool-that-you-are is the infinite Source of a mighty flowing river—the river of Life. There is no place where the pool ends and the river begins; it's all the same water. You are it. See if you can experimentally feel into the identity of the rose-gold river's Source. Is there any of 'you' in here?

Now enter the river's flow. Breathe rose-gold as you let it carry you where it will. Feel the safety and certainty of its flow. Relax your individual droplet. If you can, give yourself permission to 'go with the flow.'

A FEW HELPFUL EXERCISE TOOLS

1. Emotional processing

As old, stuck energetic patterns or dark, shadowy beliefs are released from cellular memory, more spaciousness becomes available inside the body. The more space that's created, the more room there is for the Light of divine Awareness to make itself known in our daily experience.

The following is one way of gently processing any difficult feeling or crusty old darkness that arises into conscious Awareness. This thing, whatever it may be, is just here to be acknowledged, accepted and felt. Moving through this process with unwavering love and respect gives the issue permission to release if it chooses.

EXERCISE

Together with the Light of Awareness, go within and ask respectfully if you're allowed to approach this issue. If you are not allowed (and you might not be allowed, before mutual trust has been established), don't force it.

However, if you sense the issue is saying 'yes,' (or at least, 'not no'), thank it and gently move a little bit closer. Rest here with the Light of Awareness, and feel anything that is here to be felt.

Ask if you can come closer still. If the answer is 'yes,' move closer, rest here and feel what there is to feel.

Whatever is revealed to you, your commitment must be to never turn away from what you are shown. Nothing is unlovable. With this in mind, ask if you are allowed inside it. If the answer is 'yes,' move inside the issue itself, and ask permission to feel what its experience of life is like. Your motivation here is to compassionately understand and acknowledge its discomfort. Feel its state of being as fully as you can. If doing this brings up an emotion, feel it. If its expression includes physical sensation, feel that too.

Endure any discomfort, knowing by doing so you are helping these stuck energies to dissolve soon. Thank the issue, and embrace it sincerely. In the early phases of this more intimate relationship with the subterranean self, there may be lots of issues arising that require your conscious Awareness. Take it slow. Be kind to yourself.

As you allow these old stuck energetic patterns to dissolve one by one, you naturally strengthen your connection to the inner divine wisdom that's always already here. Over time, the need for processing will diminish, and the Light of Awareness will help you determine when and whether a given issue requires it or not.

It's a good idea to always engage mindfully, respectfully, kindly and patiently, as you undertake this process. These are the very steps that develop ongoing mutual trust with all parts of the self. This is how we begin to teach ourselves unconditional love.

2. Non-reaction and non-resistance

A few years ago my young friend Leni Dubel was gifted by her spirit guides with a couple of extremely simple, straightforward exercises that help greatly with the unraveling of destructive unconscious patterns. No prior spiritual understanding or mastery is needed, to use these exercises effectively.

They are called The healing blueprint, and The arrow exercise, and they are designed to work on anything and everything, from the common cold to interpersonal relationships, to world hunger or an end to war.

The healing blueprint's focus is on non-resistance. It teaches us to welcome and accept every problem or issue as if it was our most honored guest. It can be performed any time, whether in the 'heat of the moment,' or later in meditation.

The arrow exercise teaches non-reaction to triggers, and is best performed in the moment the trigger arises. Because non-reaction and non-resistance are both so profound energetically, these exercises, although deceptively simple, bring surprisingly powerful results.

The healing blueprint (non-resistance)

EXERCISE

1. Imagine holding a sword and shield, and then setting them down off to the side. This is to represent that you are not defending against the problem, and are instead prepared to welcome it.

2. Next, imagine the issue or problem is an actual person. For instance if your issue is a flu bug, picture the flu as an actual person. Sincerely welcome and invite it into your imagined sacred meeting space.

3. Take a second to thank and then deeply love the issue. Feel this love and gratitude as sincerely as you can. If you choose to, reverently invite this issue to be your guest at a magnificent celebration held in its honor. Rejoice with it.

The whole exercise should only take 15-30 seconds. You can do this as often as you like but Leni's guides recommend that you do it at least once a day until your issue—or the suffering caused by your resistance to your issue—is resolved.

The arrow exercise (non-reaction)

This exercise helps free you of your own tendency to become triggered. It works on anything that triggers you, or makes you want to react.

EXERCISE

1. While it's occurring, simply visualize the challenging experience as a bunch of arrows that are heading toward you.

2. Choose not to let them hit their target. Direct the arrows to go around you, instead of hitting you. (Or simply stop the arrows in mid-air and let them clatter to the ground before they reach you.)

3. You have chosen not to have a reaction. You have chosen not to let your hotbutton be activated. Instead you are letting the issue or experience simply be.

Most of us don't realize we have the option not to react to a trigger. Or maybe we know we have the option, but don't feel masterful enough to make the choice in the moment when it counts. This exercise can help us experience firsthand our own power to choose against being triggered. Repetition of this exercise is like building a non-reaction muscle. The choice not to be triggered gets easier and more natural, the more often we practice it.

I worked with The arrow exercise for a short while a few years ago. The non-reaction muscle it helped me build back then has stayed with me ever since. In the Monsanto example I gave earlier, it was this skill I relied upon when I chose not to react, instead holding the neutral ideas and words in my mind, prior to breathing rose-gold through them.

3. God is the only power

Belief in God's omnipotence has been a fundamental accelerator of my own recent journey. This meditation helped me take this timeless truth beyond conceptual theory, and bring it into my own experience of life.

EXERCISE

Start by dropping within as the pure Light of Awareness, leaving behind all sense of your own history or issues. Be a blank Etch-A-Sketch in this now moment, a total question mark of a human being. Rest and breathe, with pure Awareness, pure existence, as your only identity.

Bring your focus inside the heart and solar plexus area. Affirm that you are made of the divine Light of your Source; this perfect Light is already here, now, as your own true identity. Remind yourself that intentional Awareness is automatically imbued with divine Light; this Light is intrinsically yours.

It doesn't matter whether you're able to see the inner Light or not. If you find it's a struggle to believe it, try some calculated delusionality. Temporarily set skepticism aside and see if you can allow your radiant divine identity to be true, even though it feels untrue. And to whatever degree you are able, rest as the divine Light that you already are right now.

Next, place your Awareness outside your physical self. Step outside yourself by placing your Awareness across the room, then turn and look back at yourself. (In the beginning I found this helped me step out of my usual beliefs about the power of sticky old patterns. It helped me look much more impersonally on the one who sat in meditation.)

While looking impartially at the one who sits in meditation, remind yourself the Light of divinity is all-powerful. Only the divine Light of God is real; everything that would oppose it is actually made of (very convincing) smoke and mirrors. Therefore, no pattern or circumstance can independently resist when you choose the Light of God as your identity. You notice that nothing holds any power in opposition to God. Furthermore, all patterns and circumstances are now recognized as being made of this same divine Light, existing as part of an unbroken field of all-that-is.

This reminder, in combination with the outside-the-body viewing of myself, helped me see my body-mind-energy field as pure divine Source, and not as the victim of sticky inner forces or patterns that 'won't let go of me.'

With repeated exposure to divine Awareness as the Light I am, a knowing of inner freedom began to come alive. And with this knowing, a great many persistently held secrets thawed out and released.

*   *   *   *

A note about spiritual alchemy, which is closely related to the above-mentioned knowing of inner freedom:

In a sense, every exercise in this book helps prepare the way for spiritual alchemy. Yet no exercise is included here for spiritual alchemy itself, because each of us approaches it in our own unique way. The best I can do is describe my own process with it, as a springboard to help you find yours.

As I've said, it all starts with the firm (delusional) decision that God is the only power. When I bring a roadblock issue to this foundational belief, I agree to witness the issue without any of the historical ideas I've always wrapped around it. (This agreement not to be impressed by the roadblock's invincibility feels highly delusional. Invincibility, after all, is what makes it a roadblock.)

I simply let the issue be. As I let it be, it is revealed as being one hundred percent made of God. Already perfect. I, the witness, am automatically recognized as being the same. The perfection of God is witnessing the perfection of God. Nothing is wrong. Nothing ever could be wrong. God is.

I rest inside the issue *as* the omnipotence of God witnessing itself. It is at this point that the obstacle, or rather my lifelong belief in it, is recognized as a creaky old obsolete structure. I realize I used to need it, to help me believe in my own smallness. But now I no longer do. So I thank it for its service, and I let it stay or go as it chooses. Either way, its reign is coming to an end.

Those are the steps I take. Yours may be different. Spiritual alchemy is a process that flows with divine inspiration in each moment, in a way that's perfectly suited to each one's own journey. As you learn to receive and act on those heavenly prompts, your own alchemical liberation (perhaps looking nothing like mine) will unfold before you in all its magnificent glory.

*   *   *   *

NOTES

NOTES

Carrie is the multi-award winning author of four books:
The Fricken Map is Upside Down
Tastes Like God
The Enlightenment Project
Long Time No See

She lives in southwest England with one husband,
two cats, and a great many bugs, birds,
cauliflowers and trees.